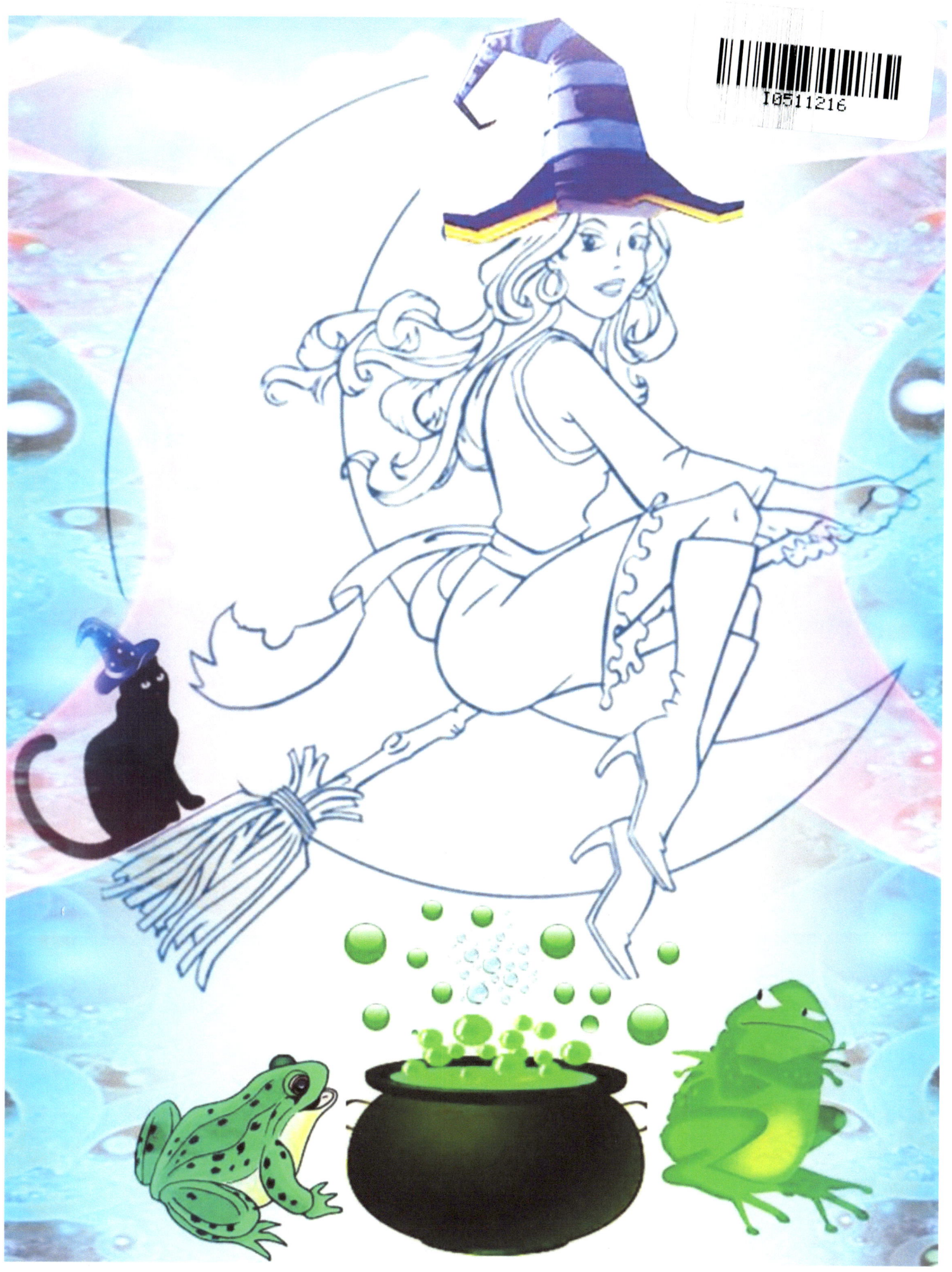

I0511216

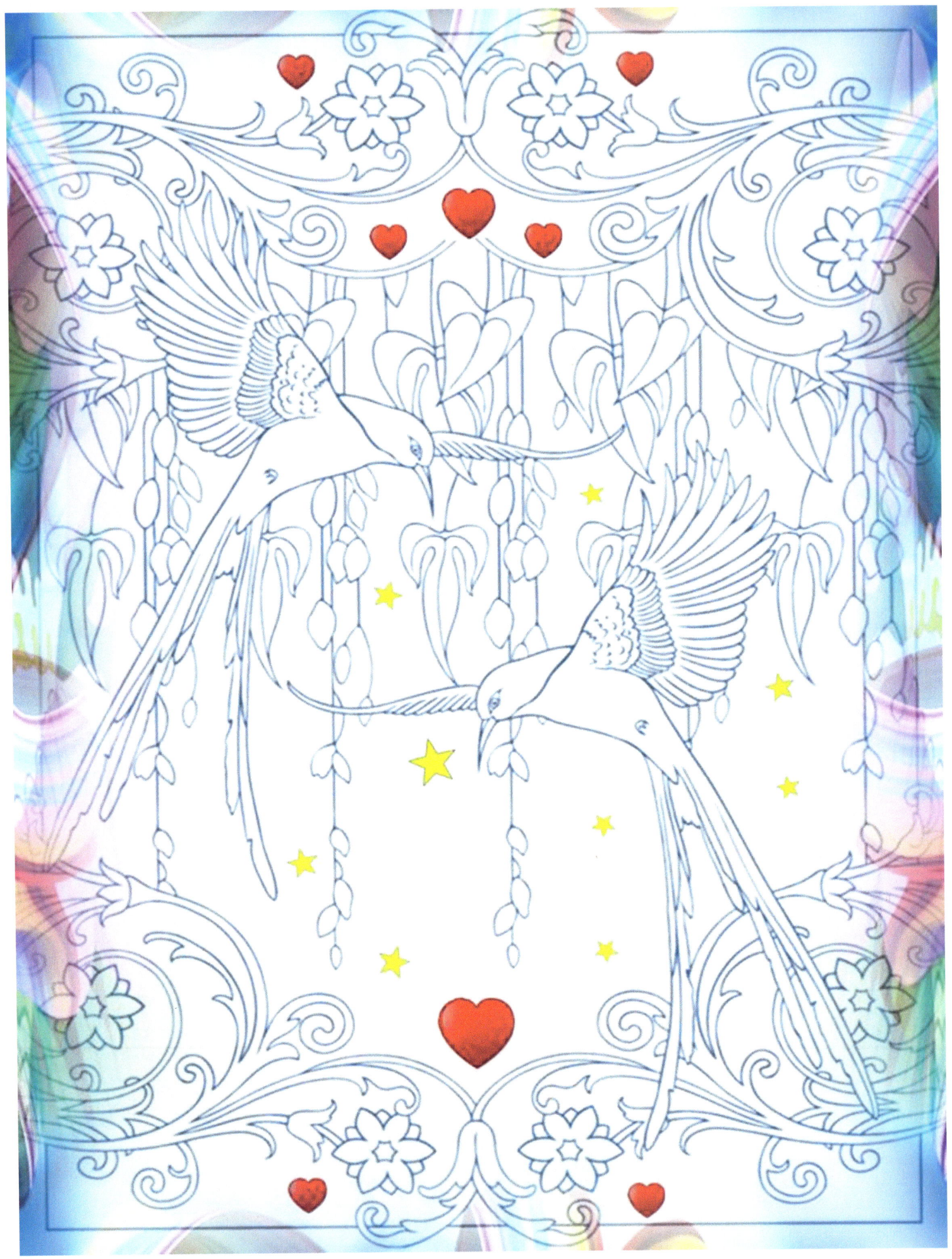

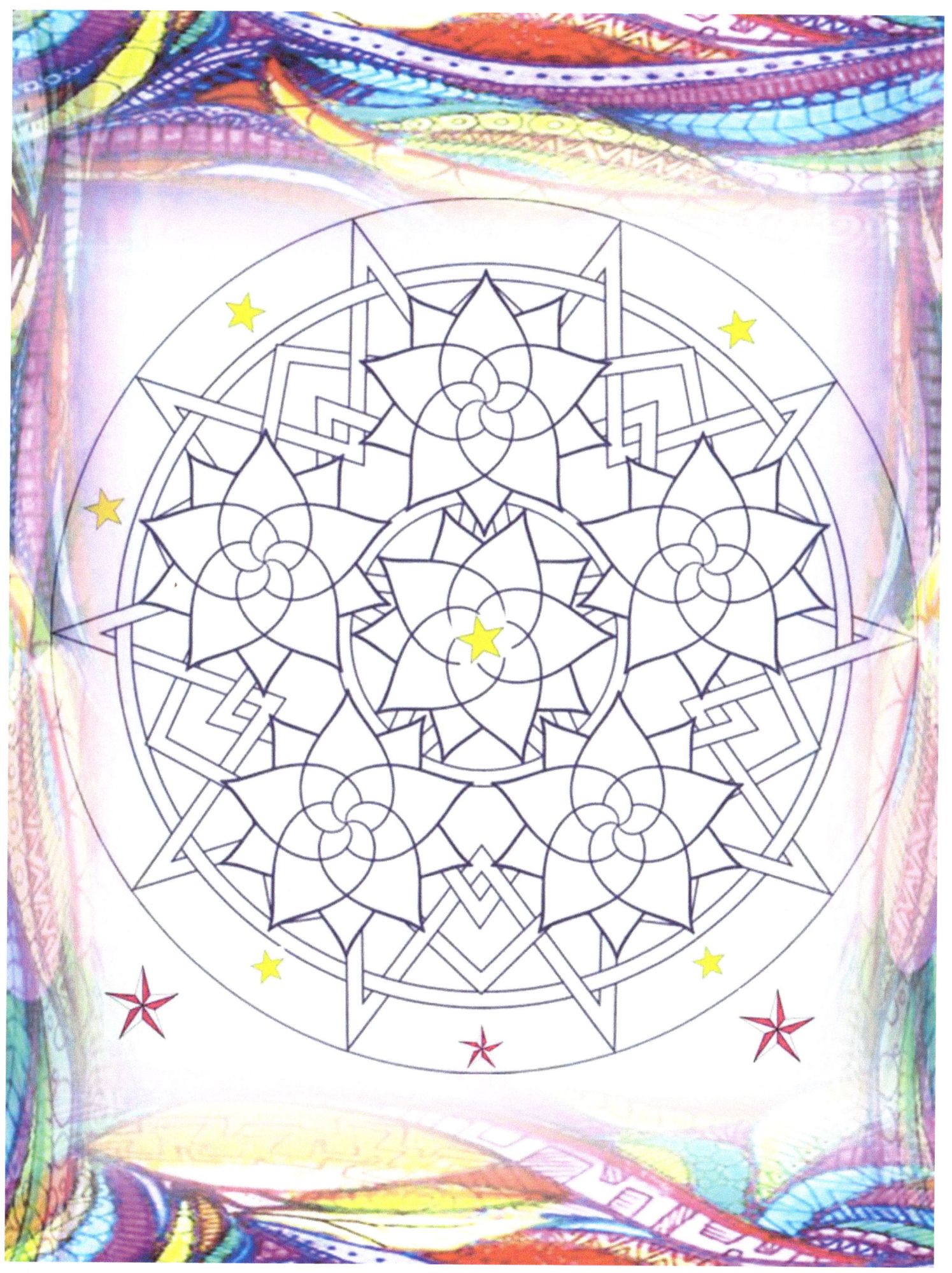

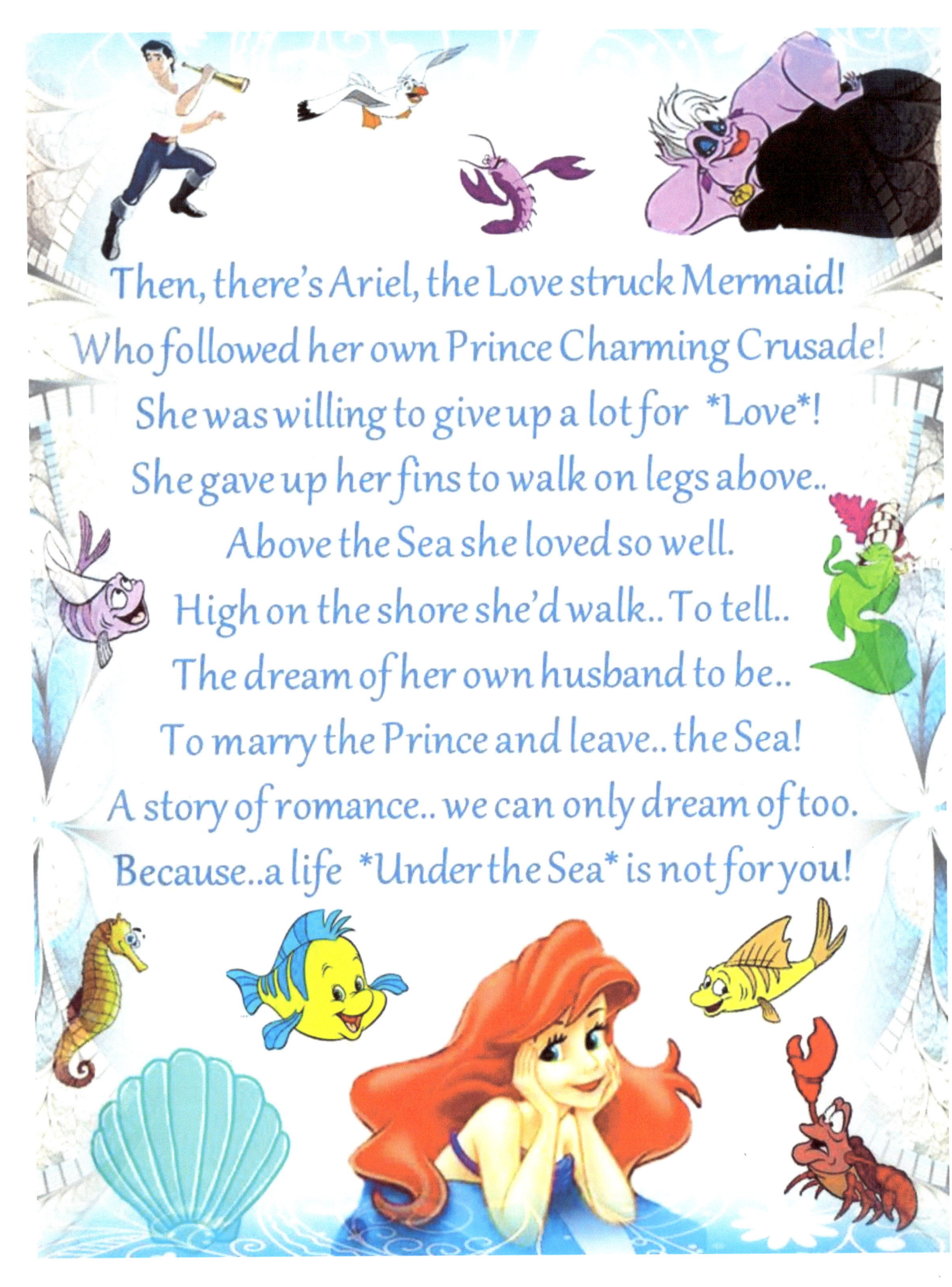

Then, there's Ariel, the Love struck Mermaid!

Who followed her own Prince Charming Crusade!

She was willing to give up a lot for *Love*!

She gave up her fins to walk on legs above..

Above the Sea she loved so well.

High on the shore she'd walk.. To tell..

The dream of her own husband to be..

To marry the Prince and leave.. the Sea!

A story of romance.. we can only dream of too.

Because..a life *Under the Sea* is not for you!

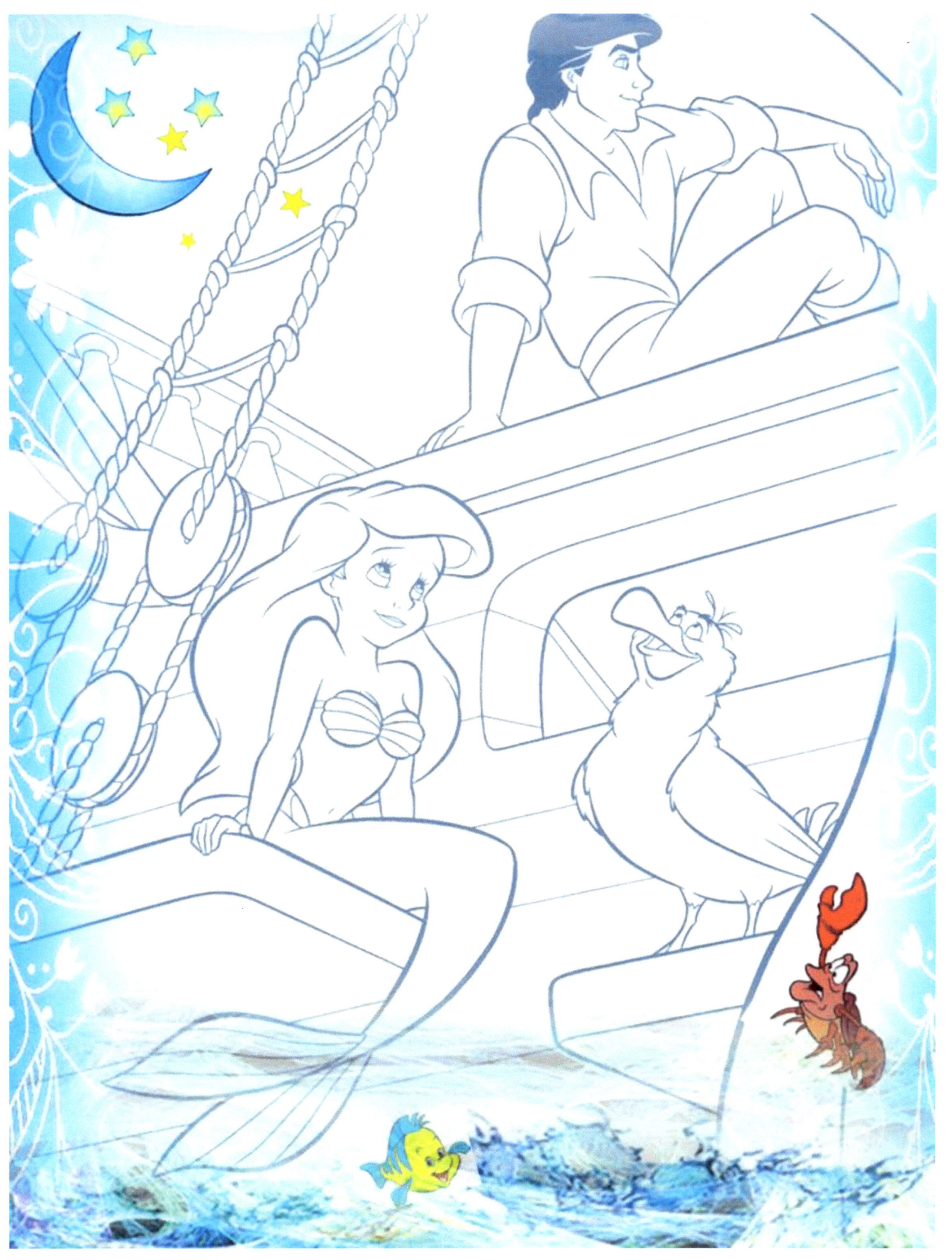

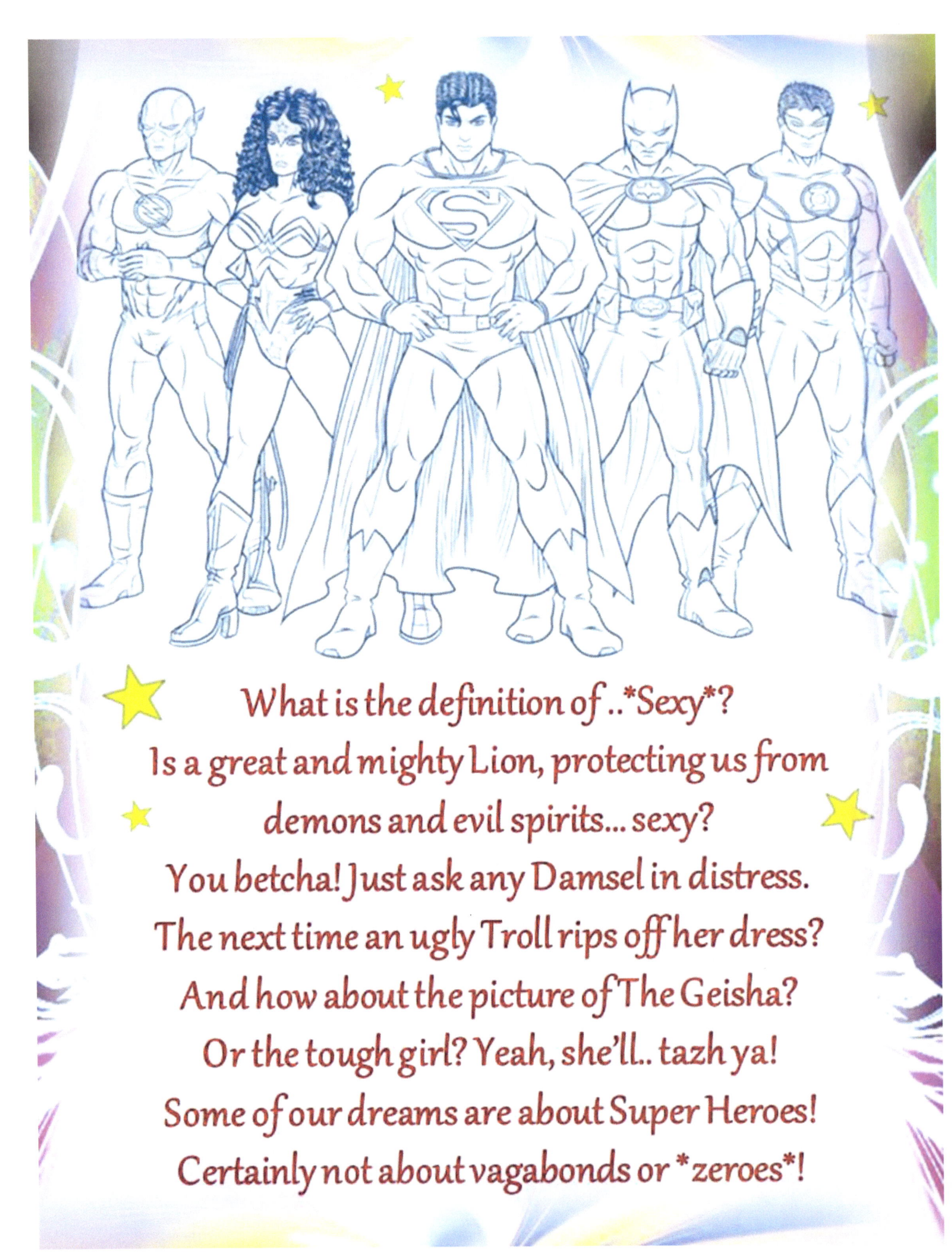

What is the definition of ..*Sexy*?
Is a great and mighty Lion, protecting us from
demons and evil spirits... sexy?
You betcha! Just ask any Damsel in distress.
The next time an ugly Troll rips off her dress?
And how about the picture of The Geisha?
Or the tough girl? Yeah, she'll.. tazh ya!
Some of our dreams are about Super Heroes!
Certainly not about vagabonds or *zeroes*!

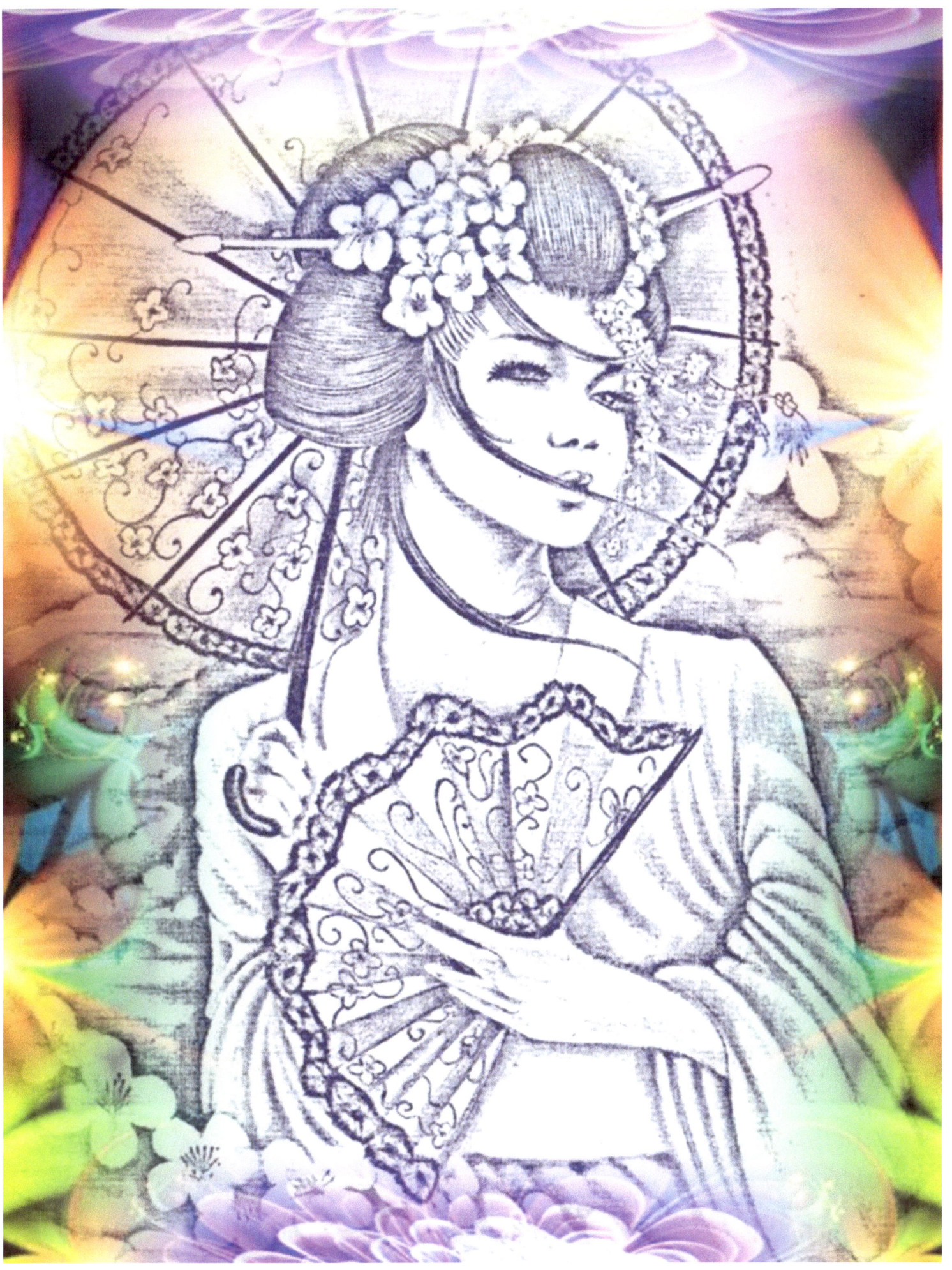

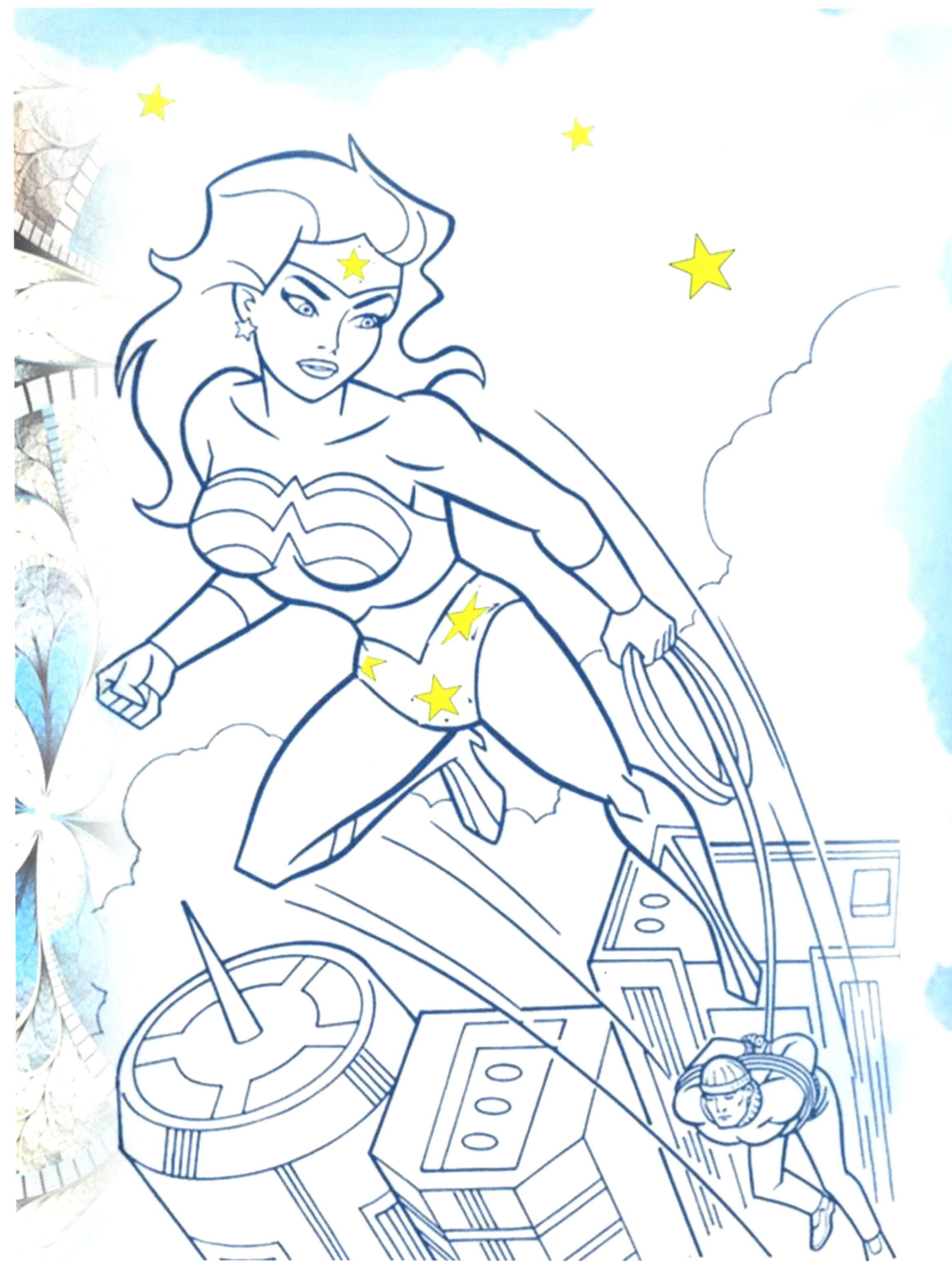

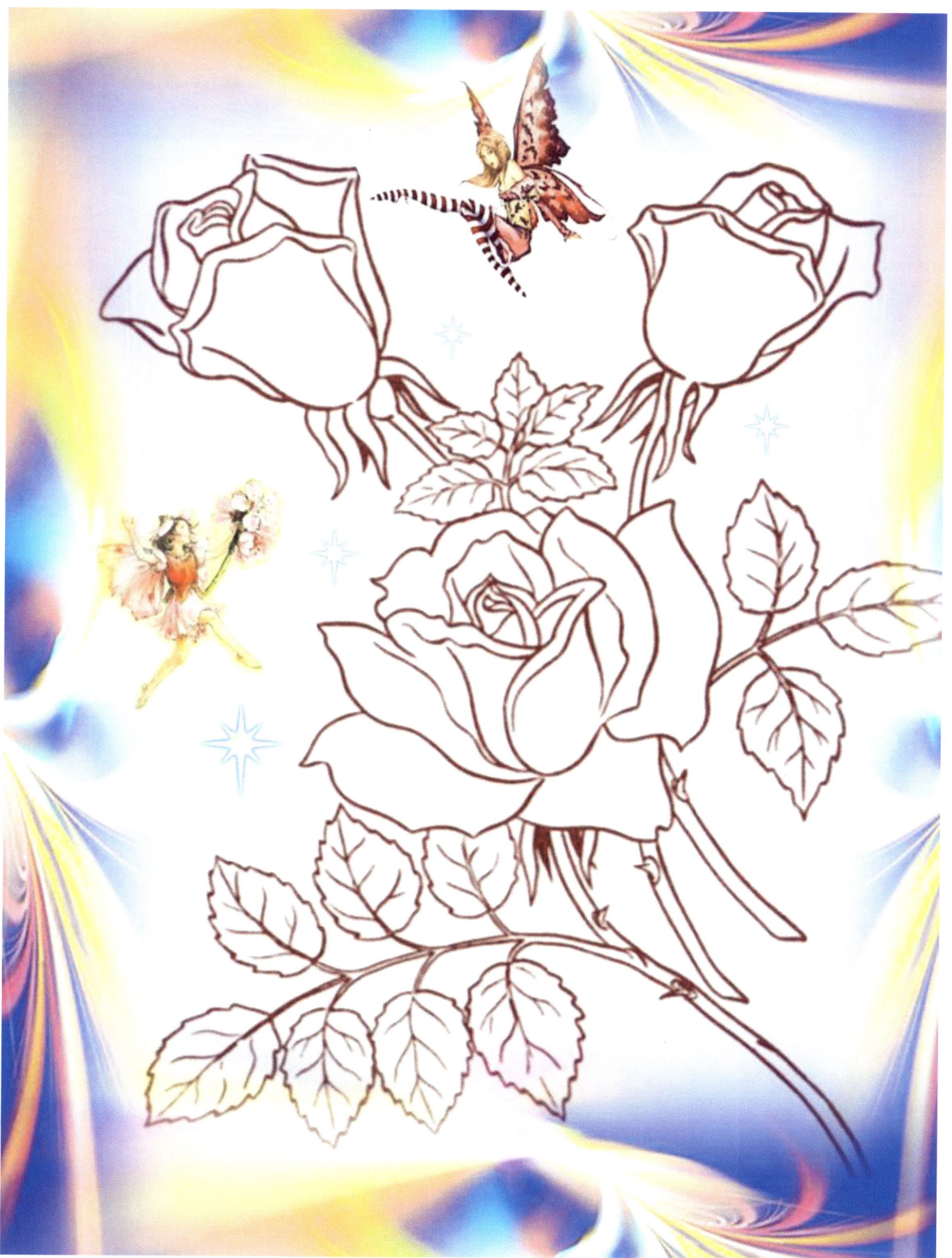

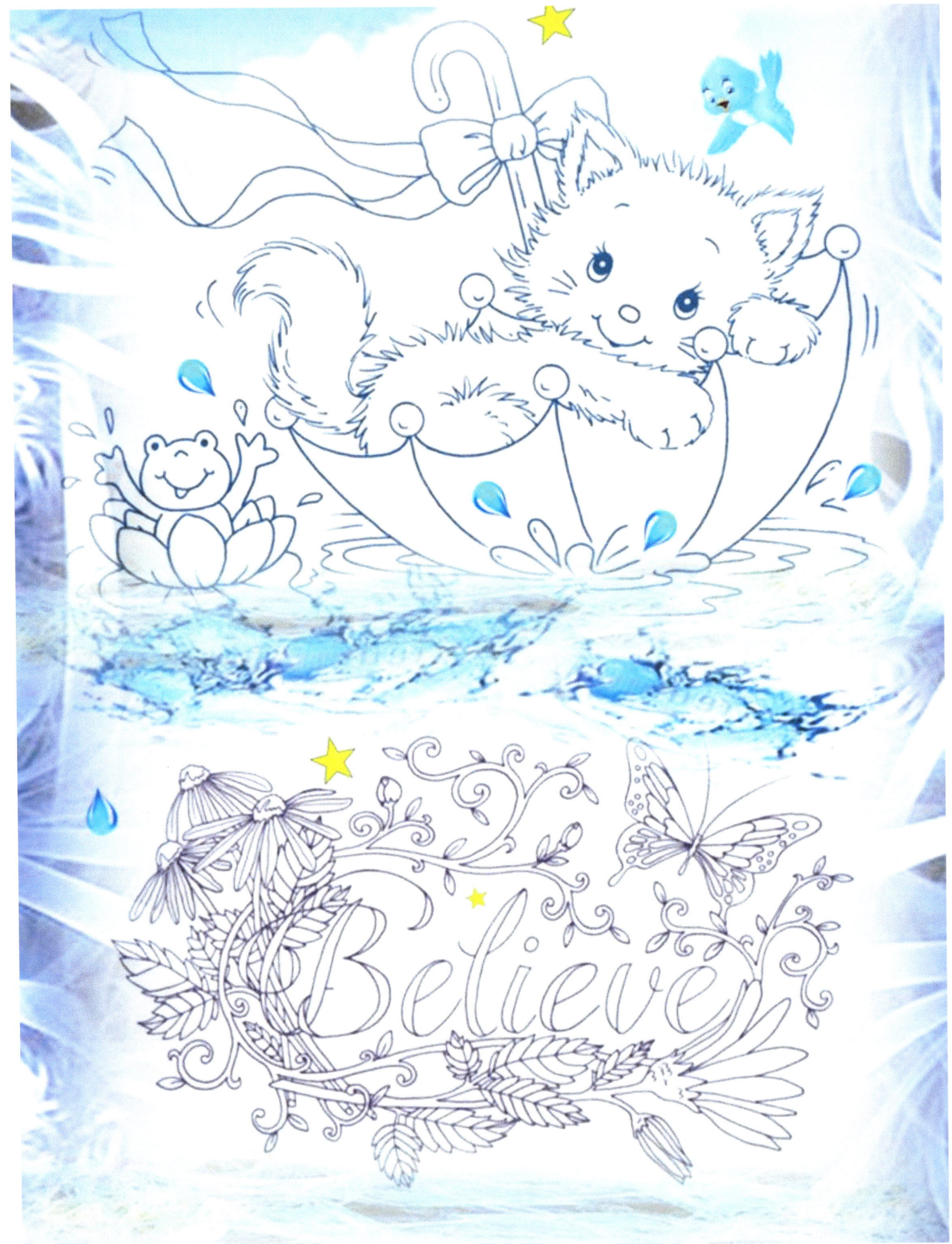

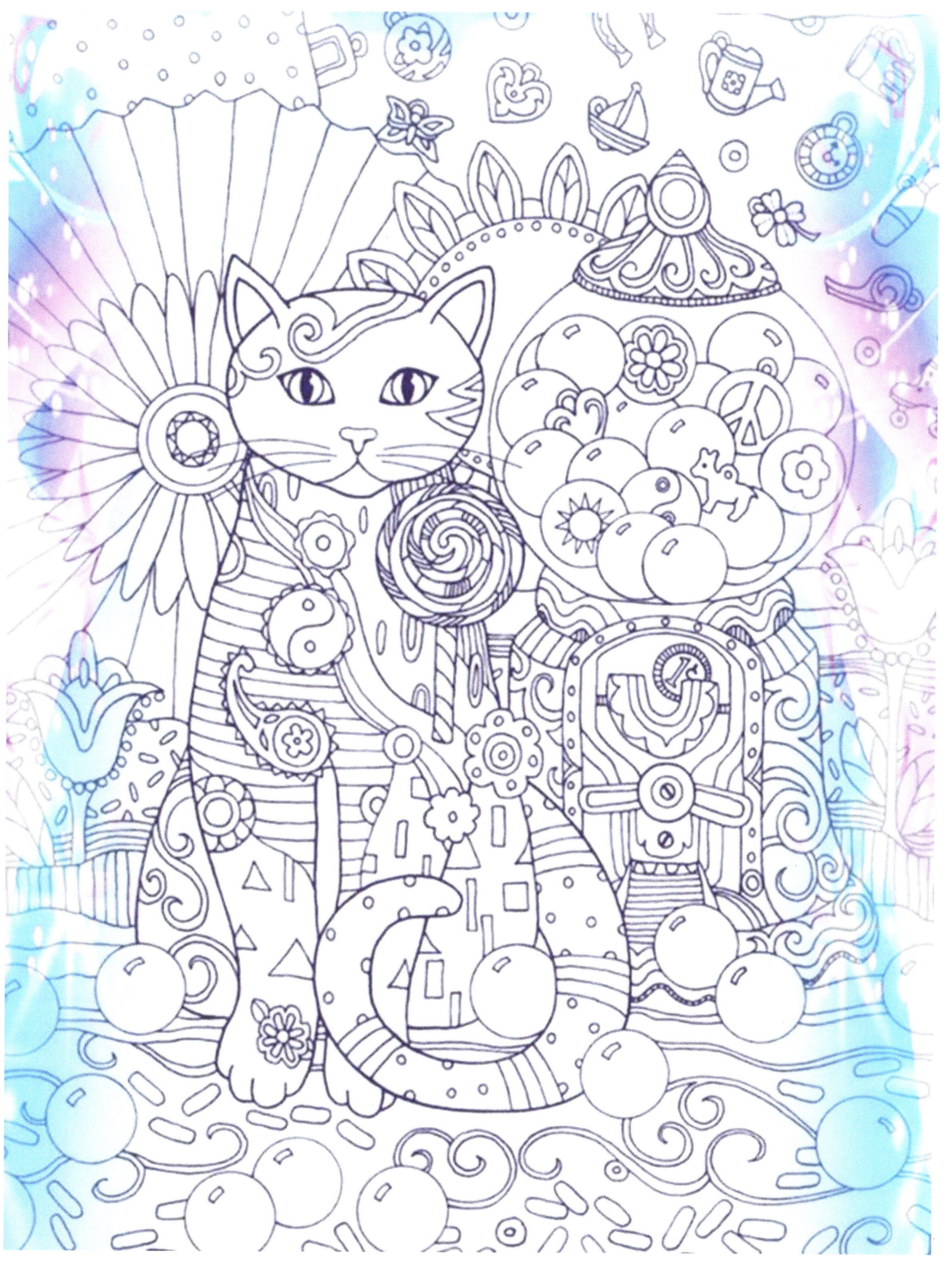

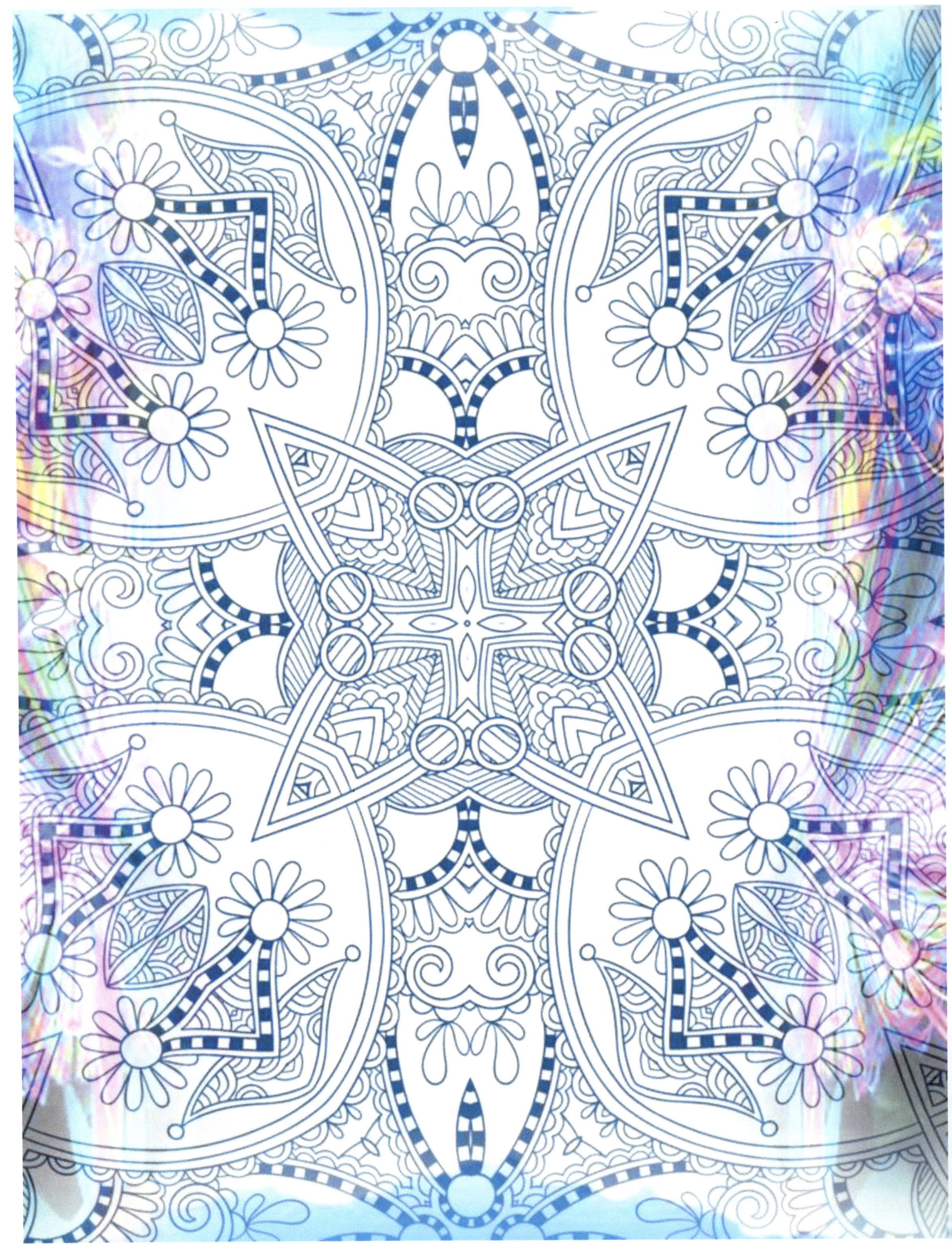

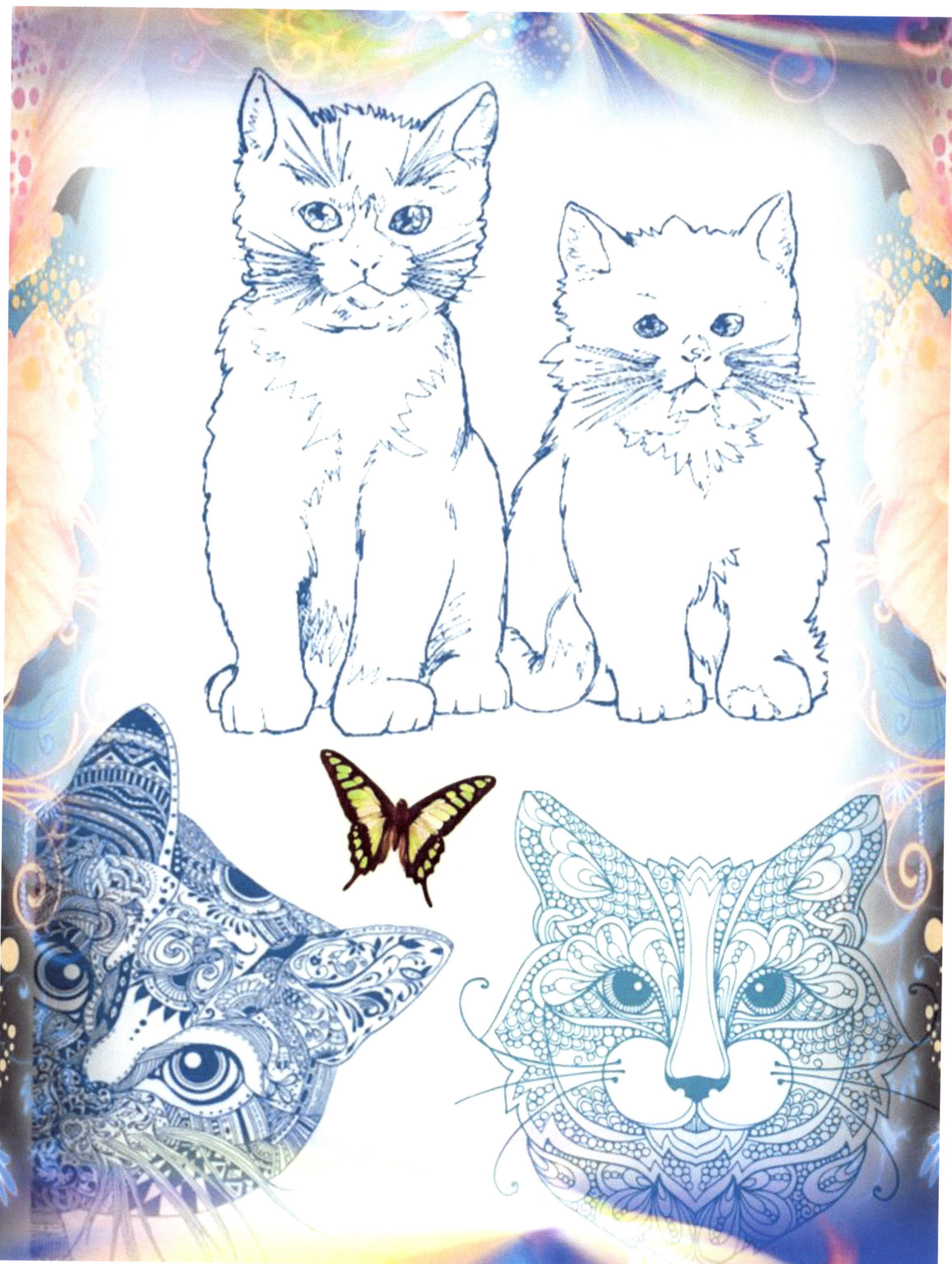

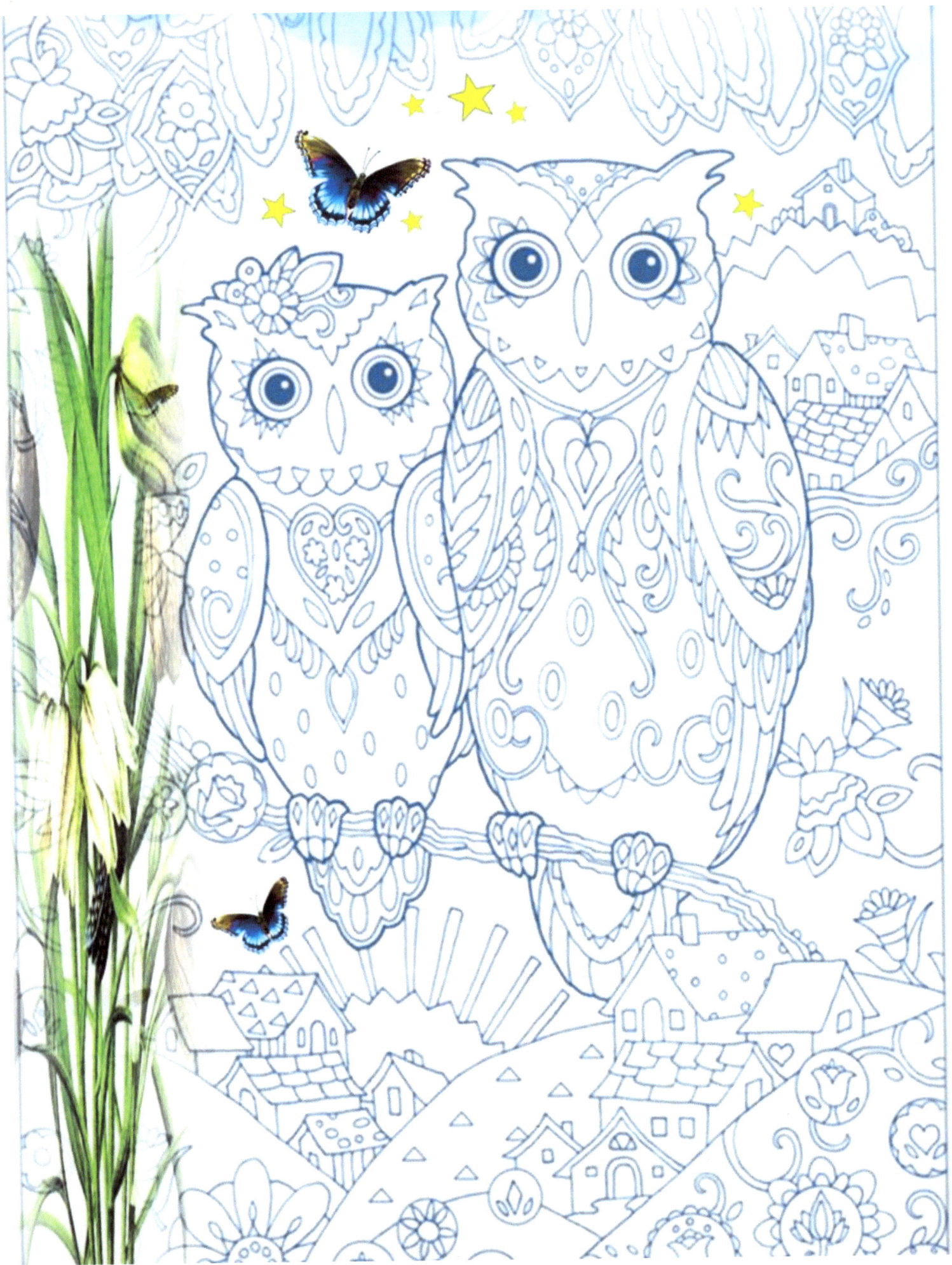

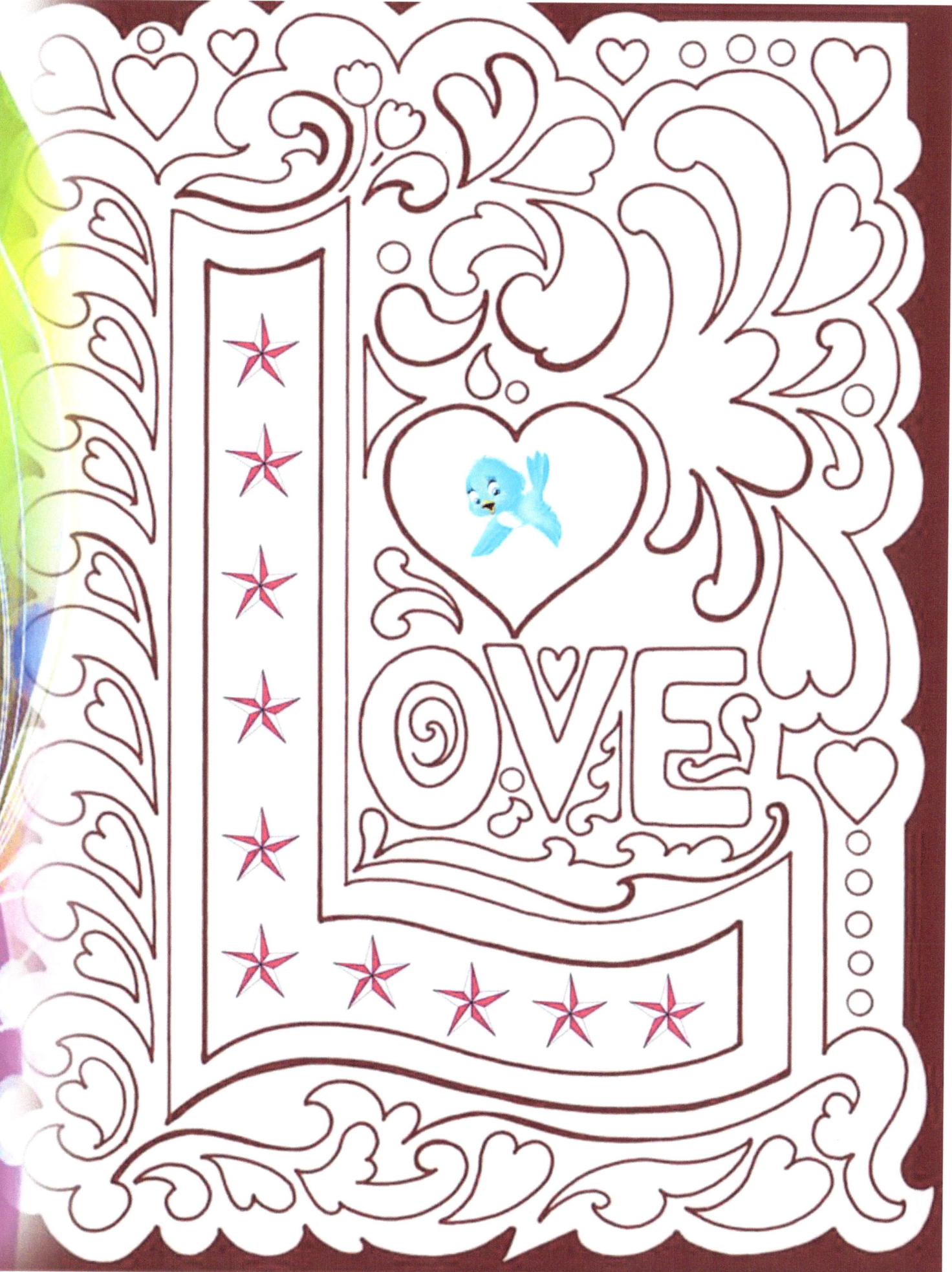

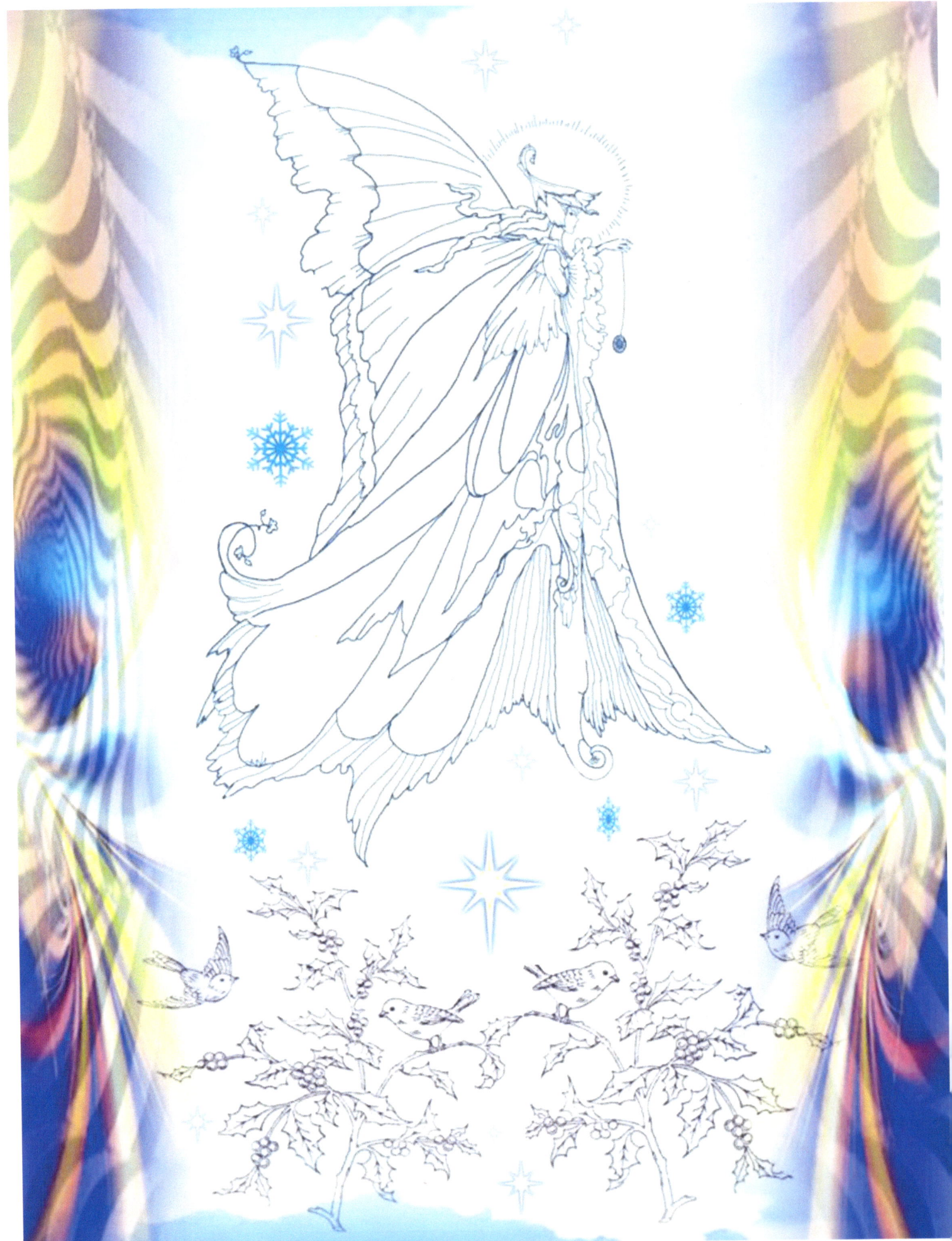

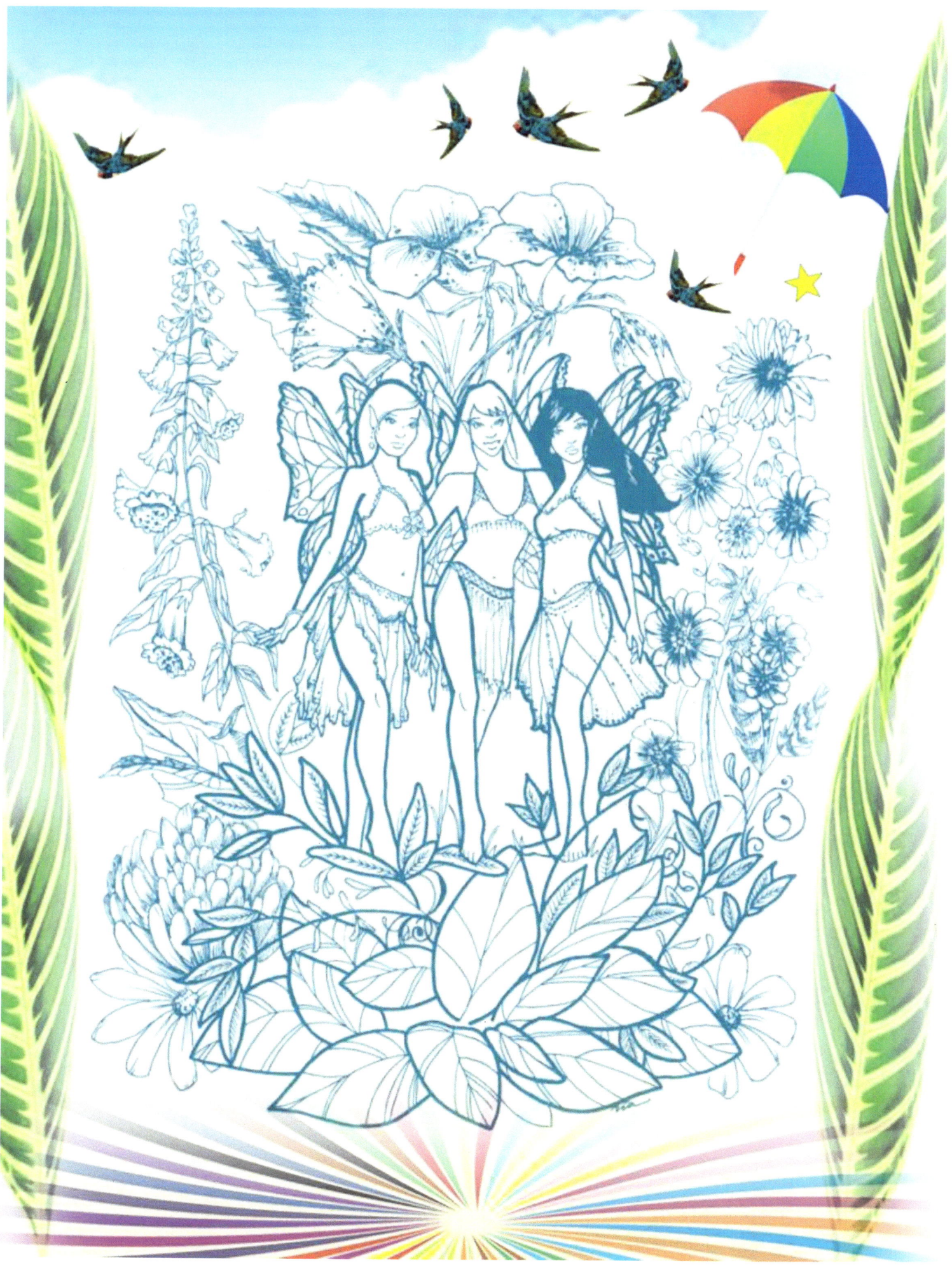

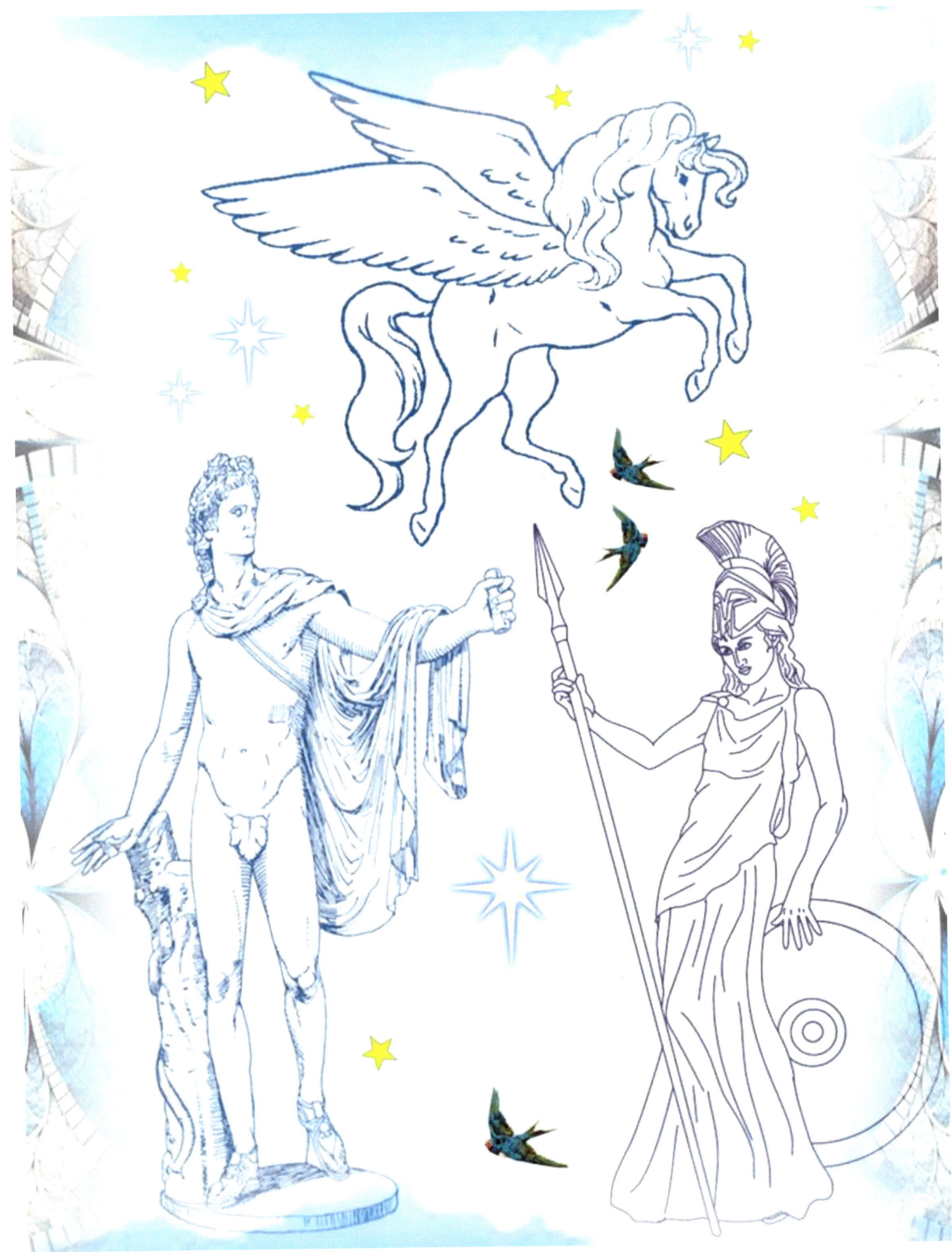

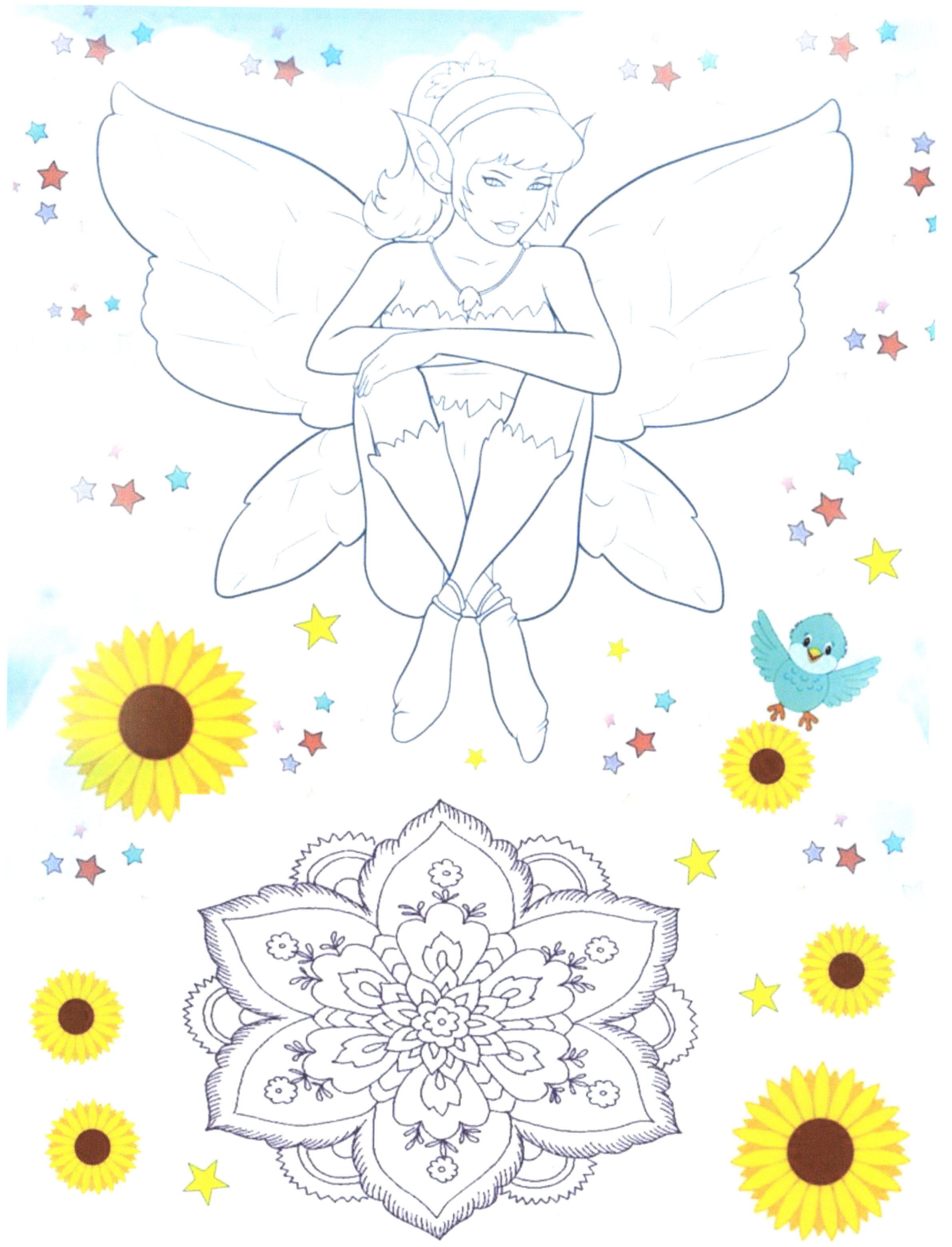

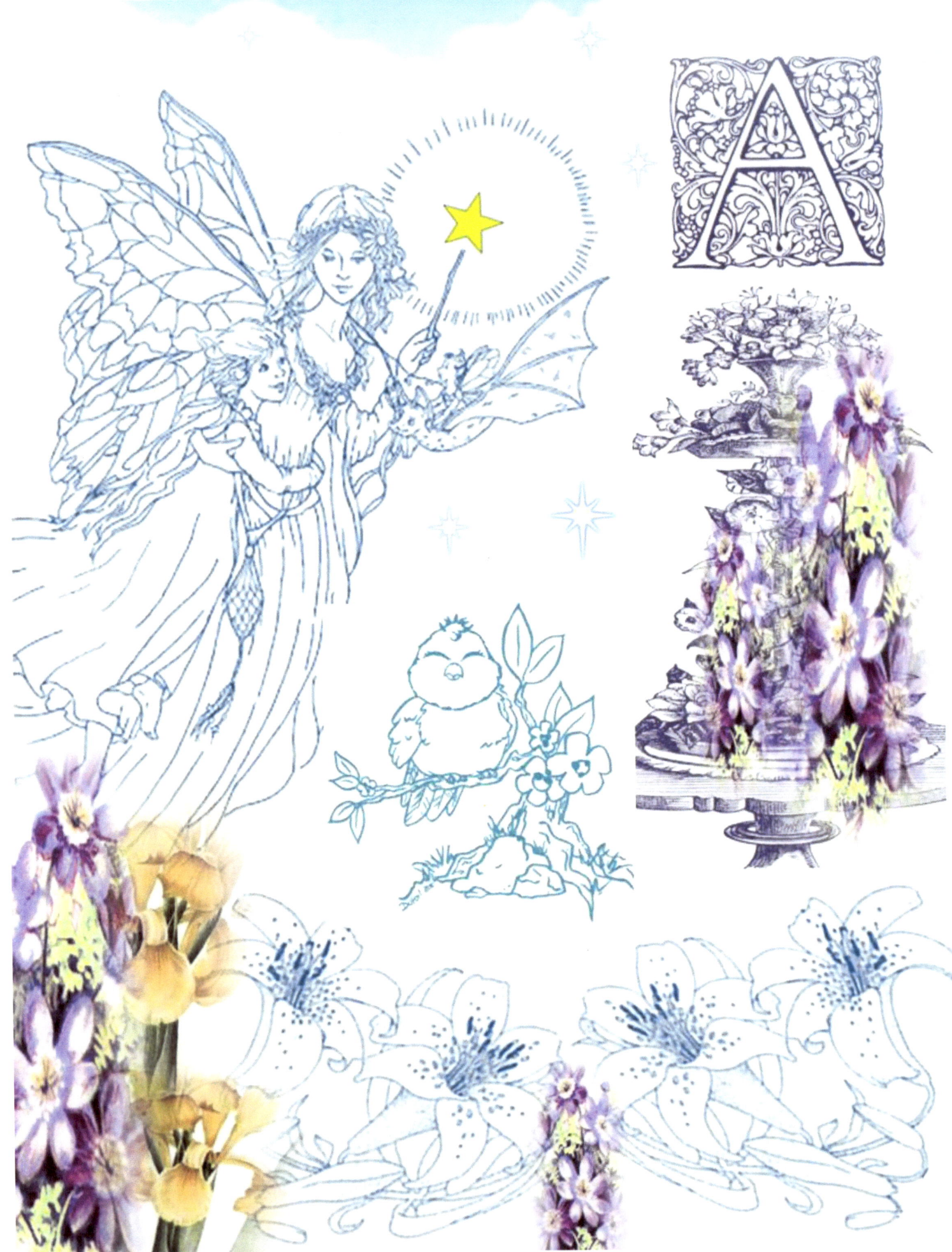

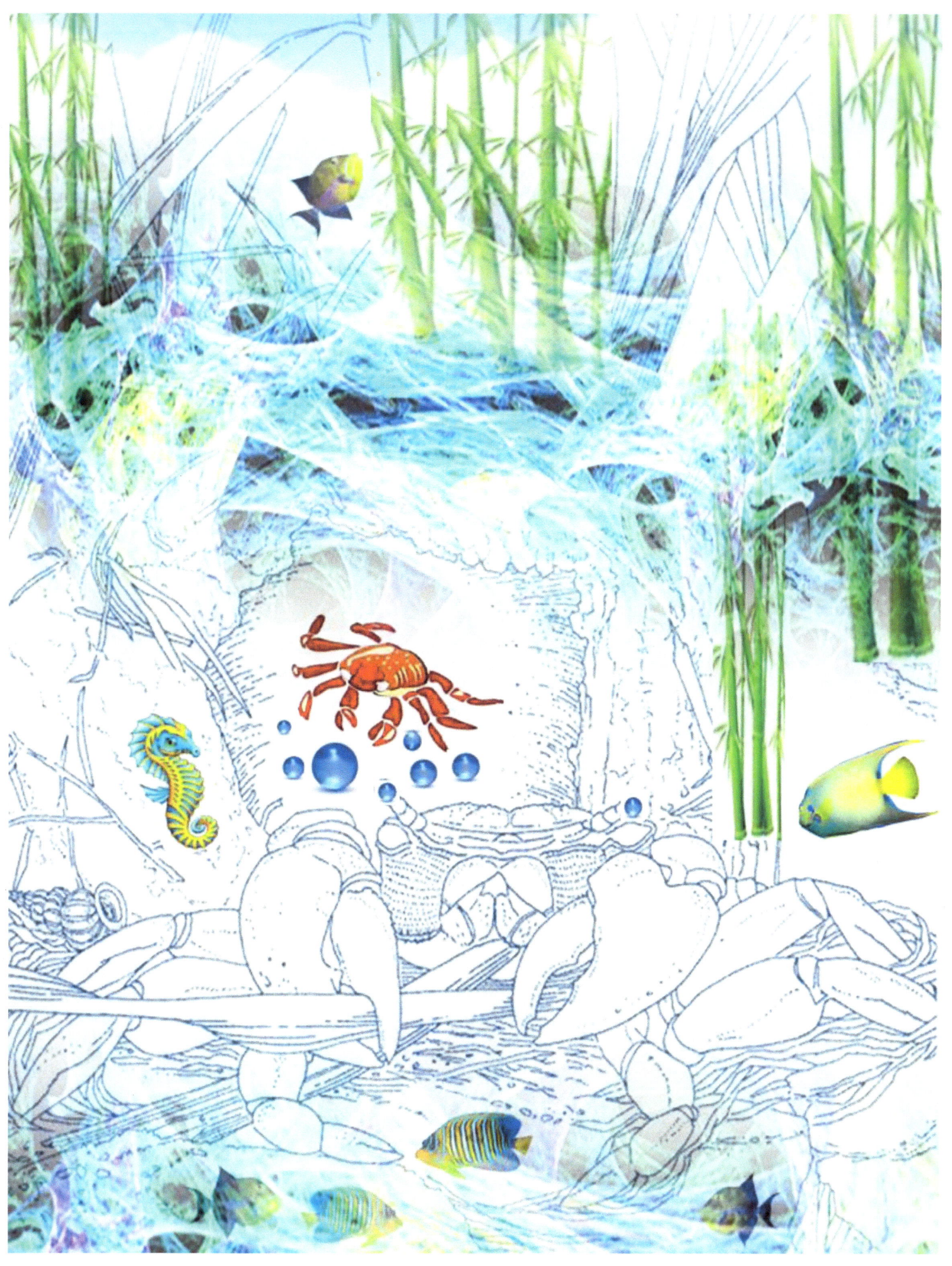

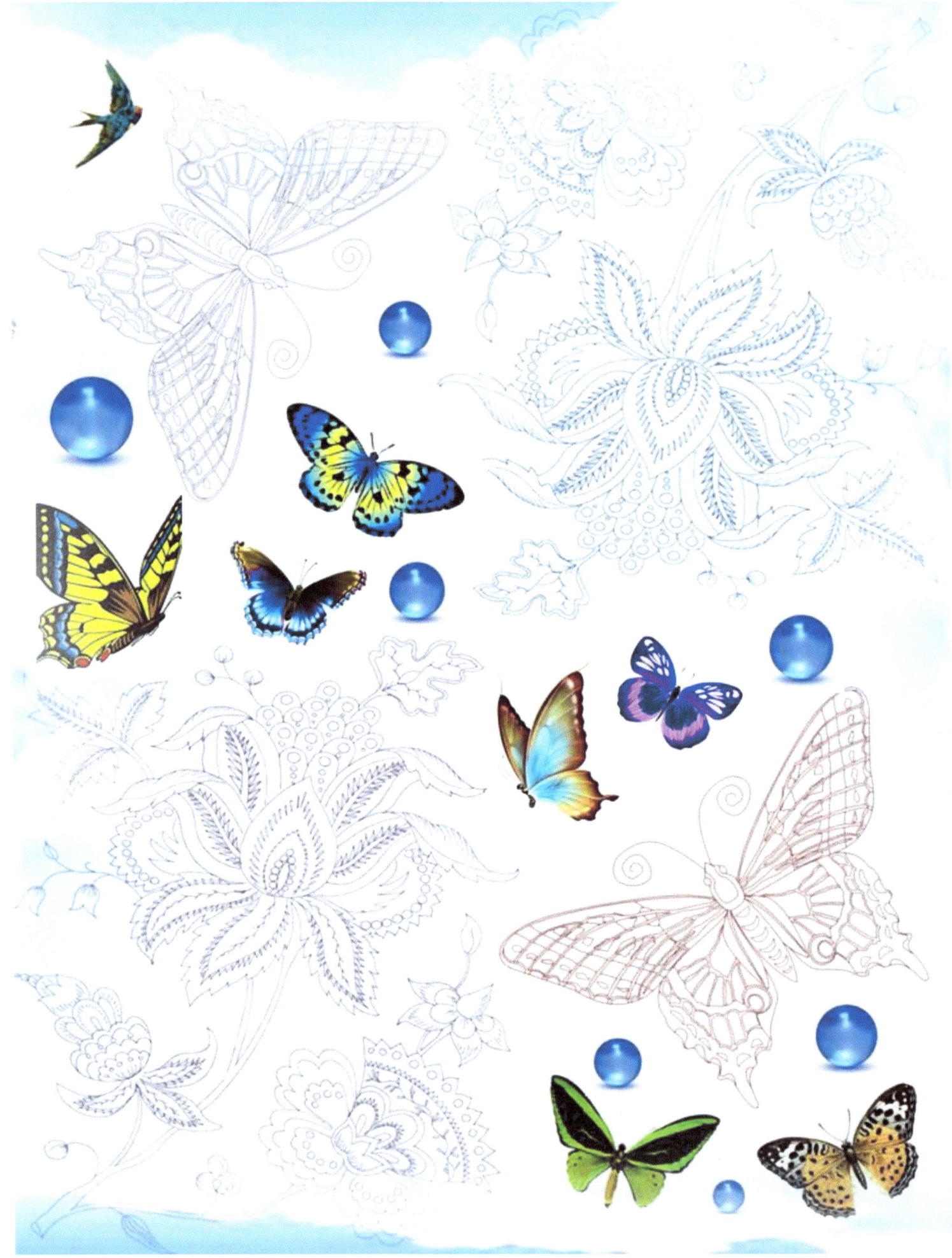

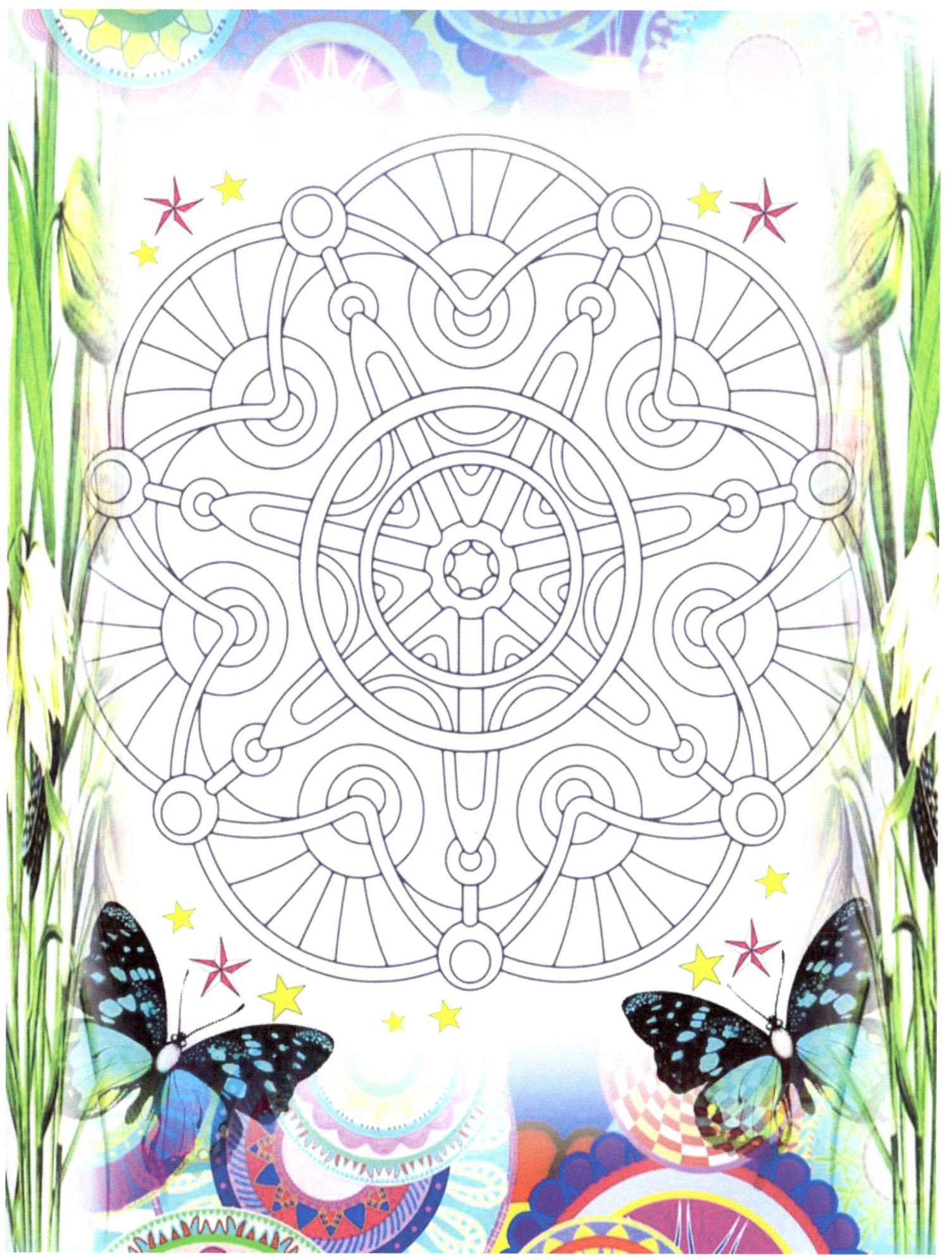

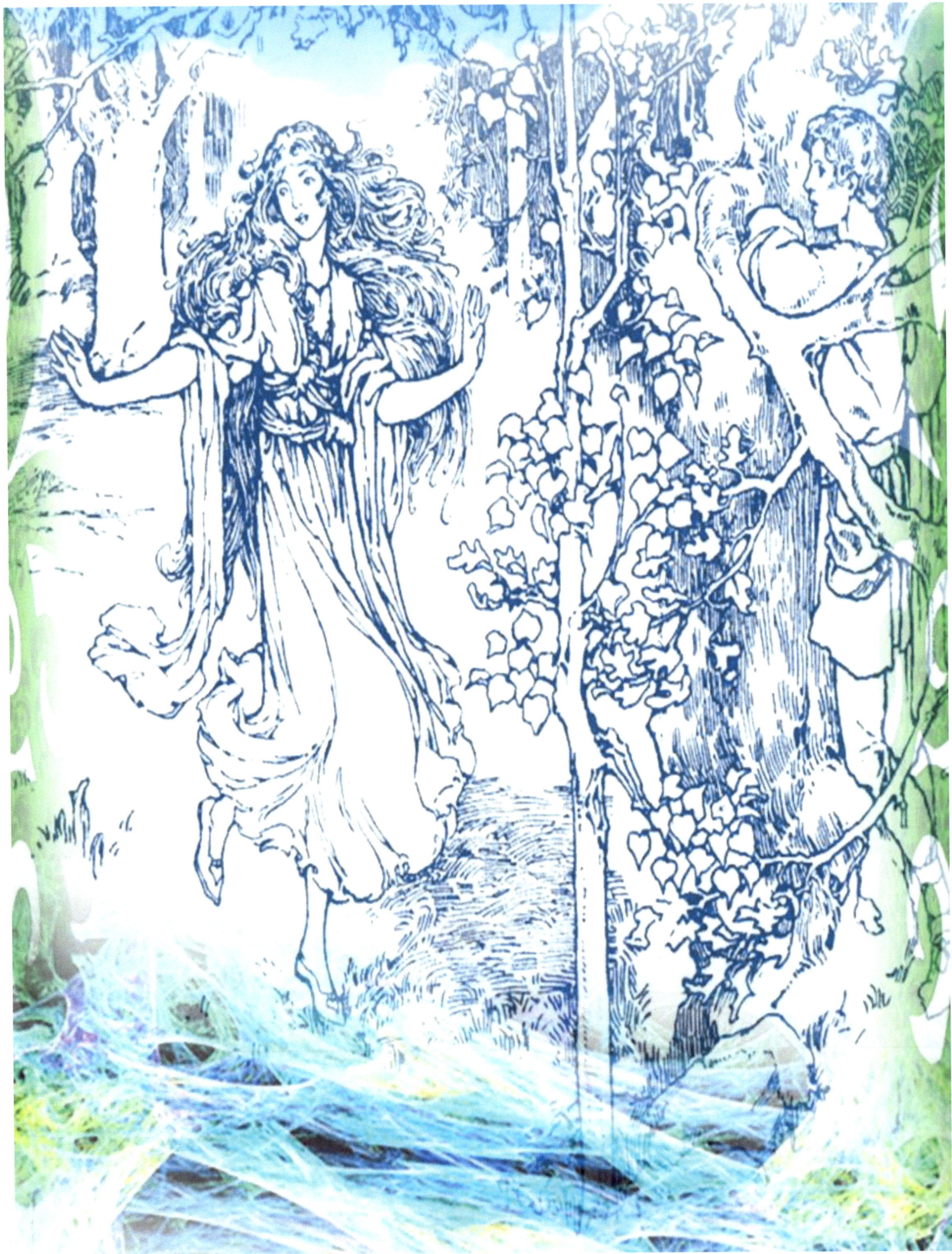

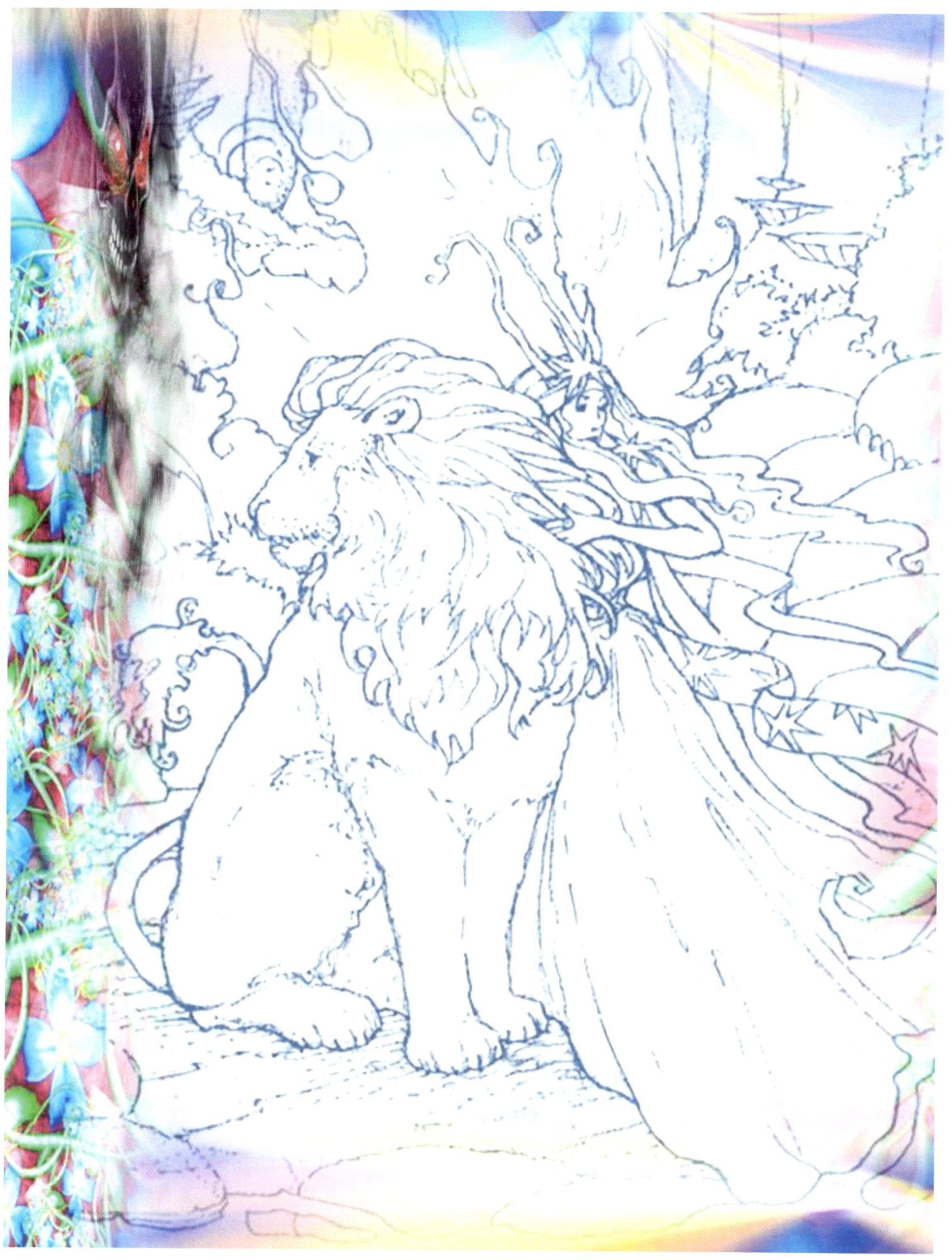

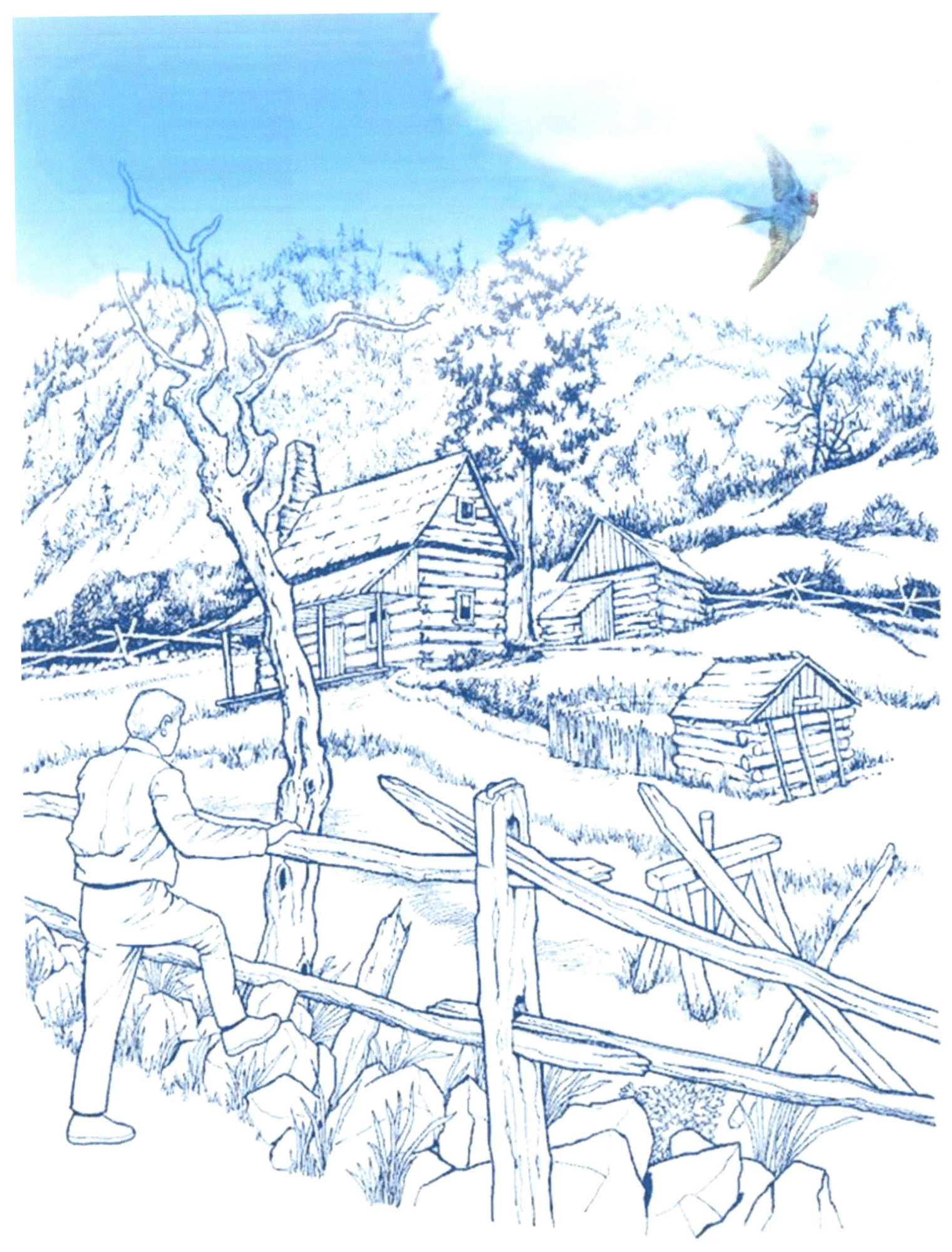

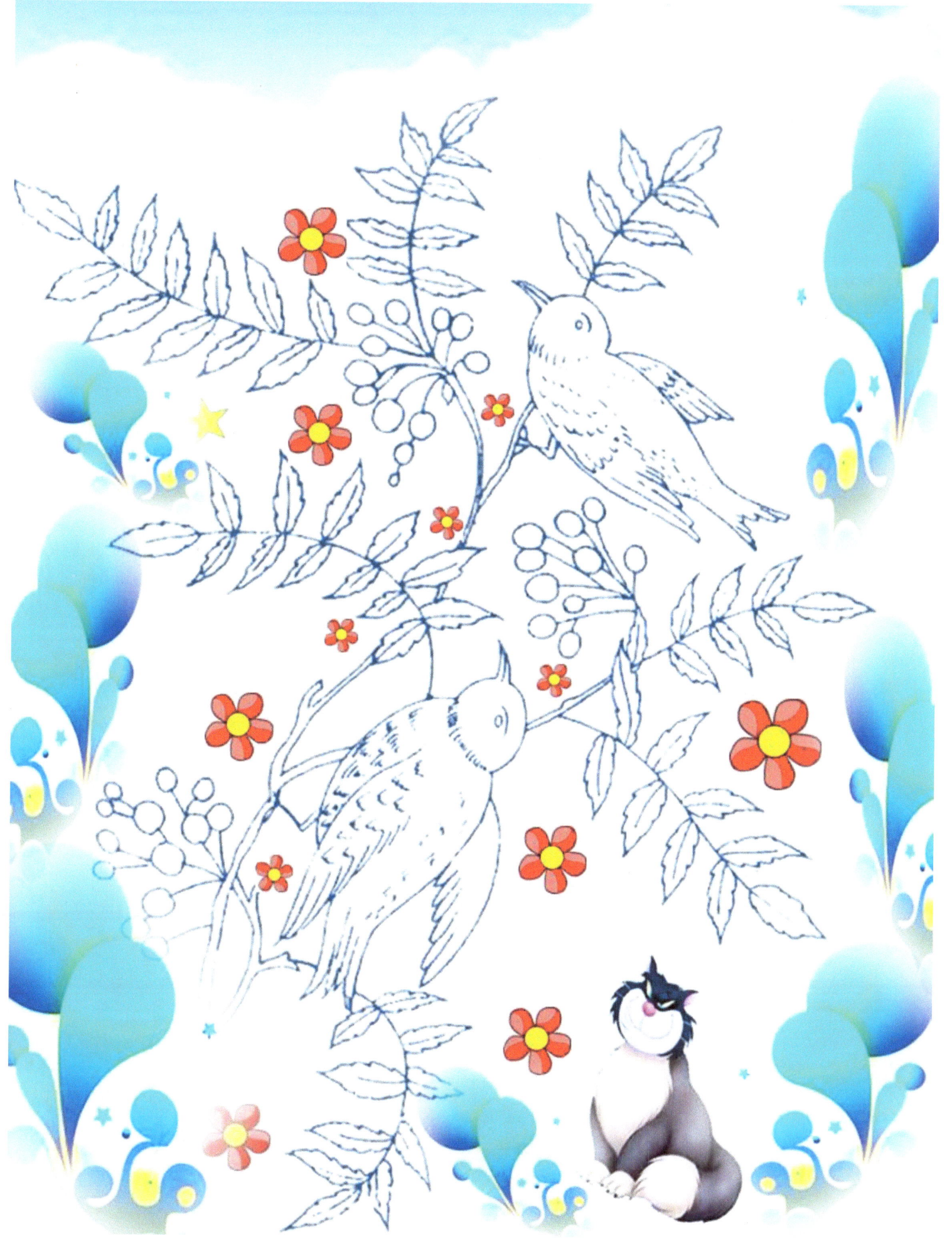

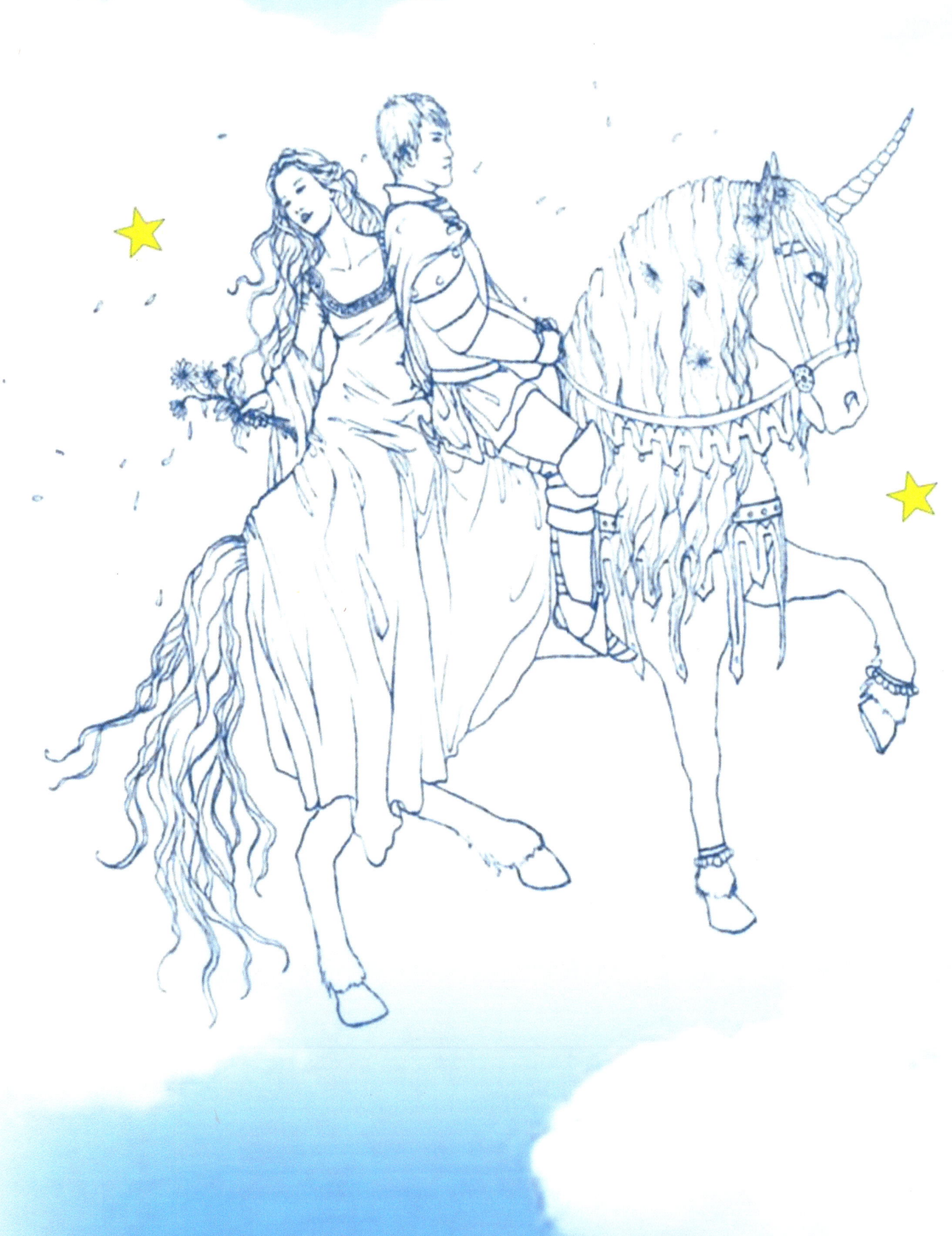

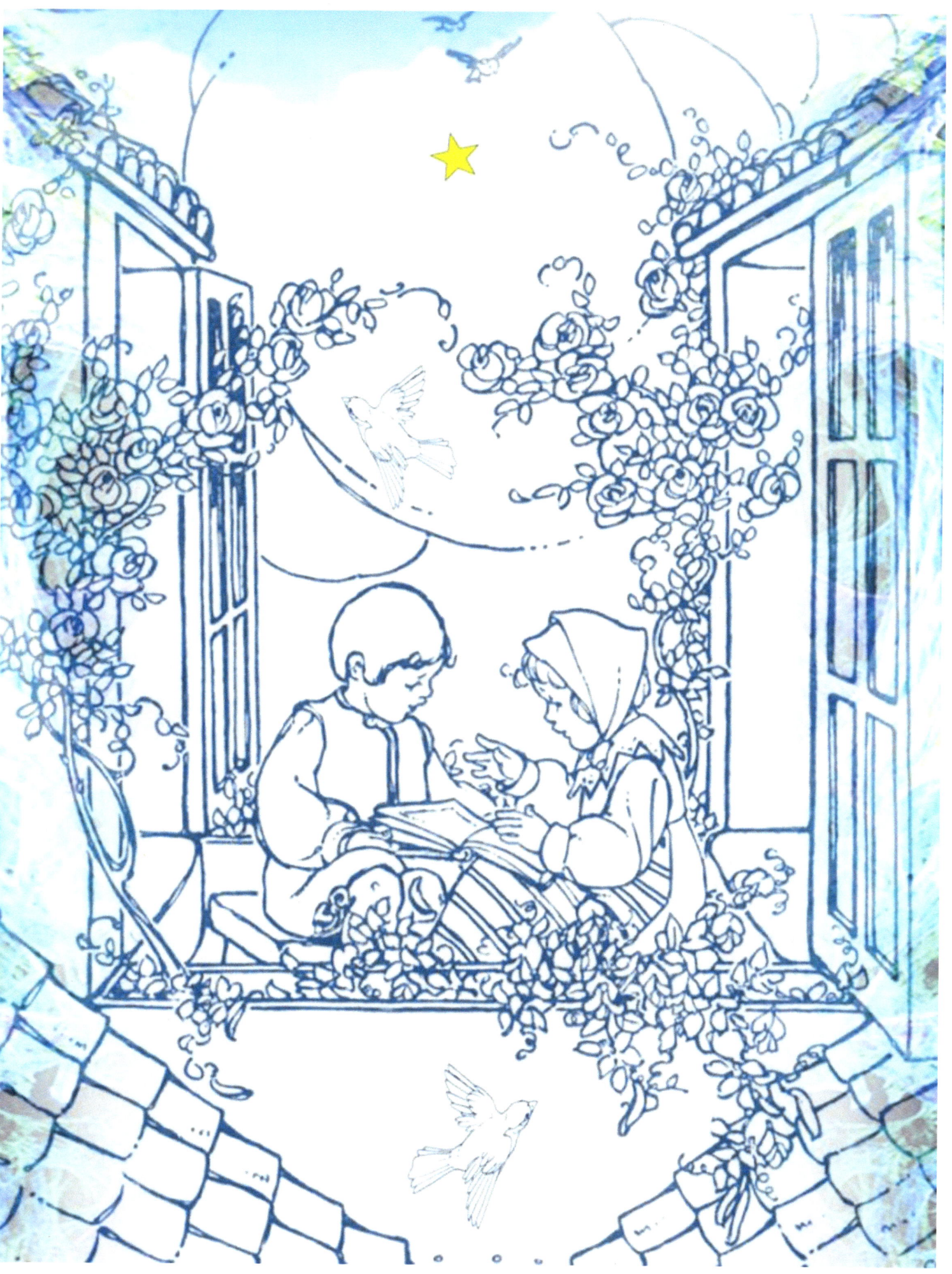

Babies..we see ourselves as we wish we were..
We see ourselves in a way we hope that we
were..The joy and peace of the innocent is
overwhelming. Tears always come to my eyes
when I see them ...More.. when I touch their
little hands and faces.. Their smiles are always
real and always welcoming. Babies.
They emanate the love we long for.
They generate the happiness we wish for.
Blessed are the babies born on this day..
The first day of the new year.
Happy Birthday Angel 2017!
The ability to feel and know this innocence is
gone forever. Yet we can hold on to the visage of
others knowing it and showing it ..to us.

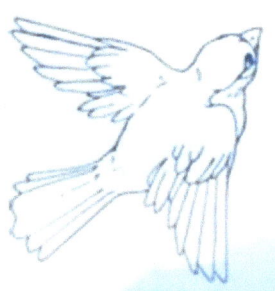
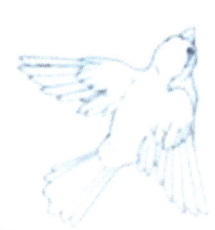
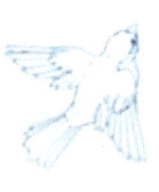

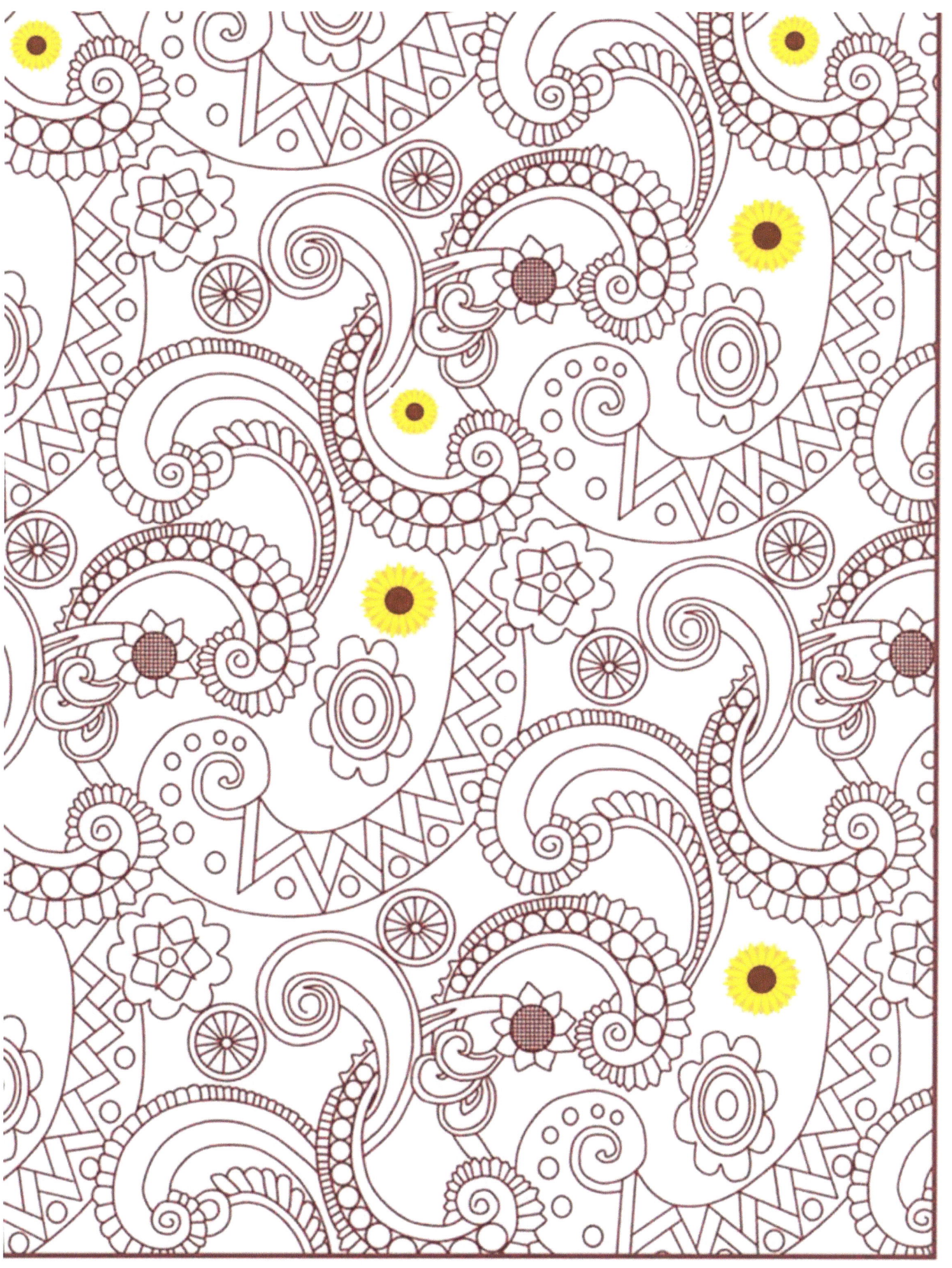

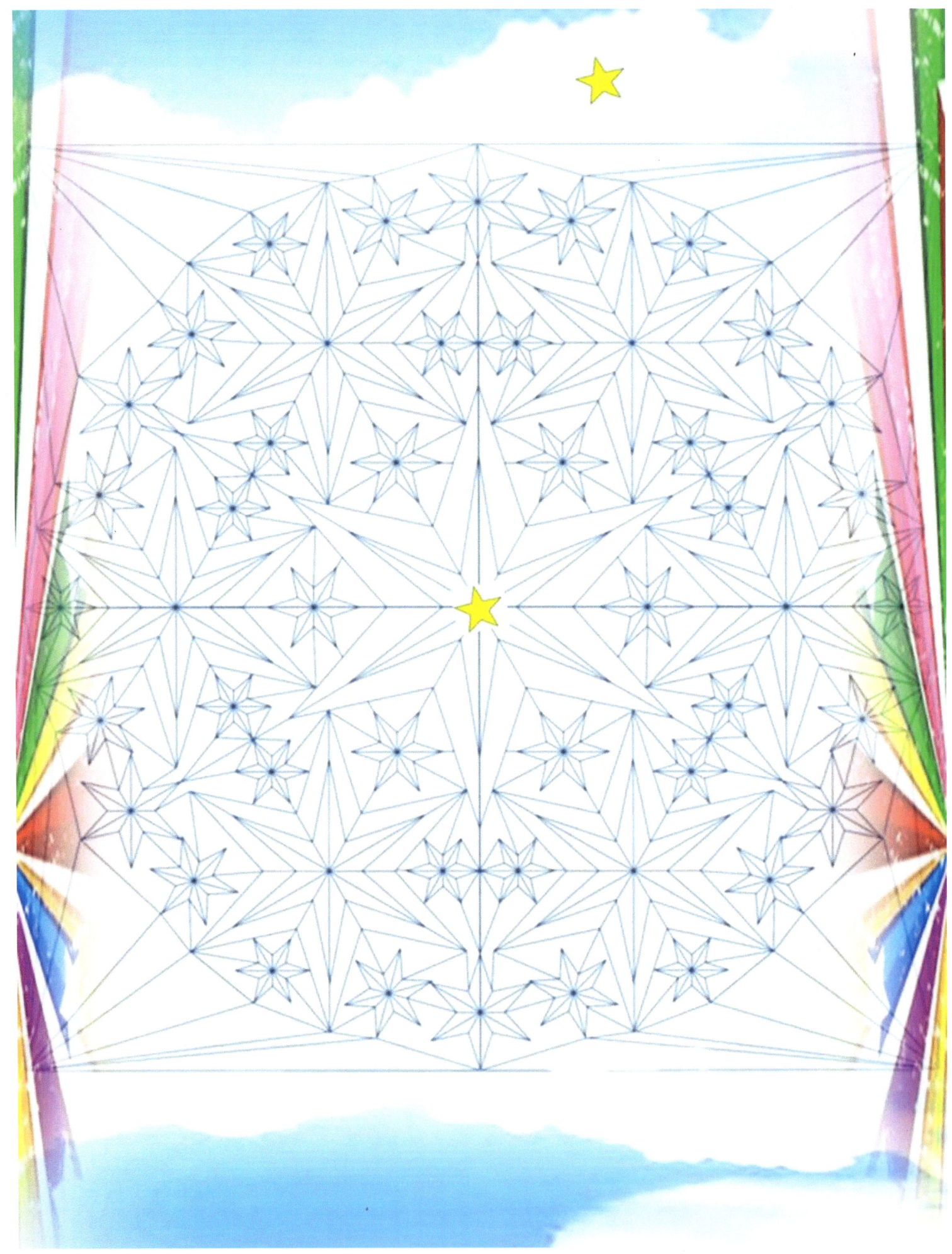

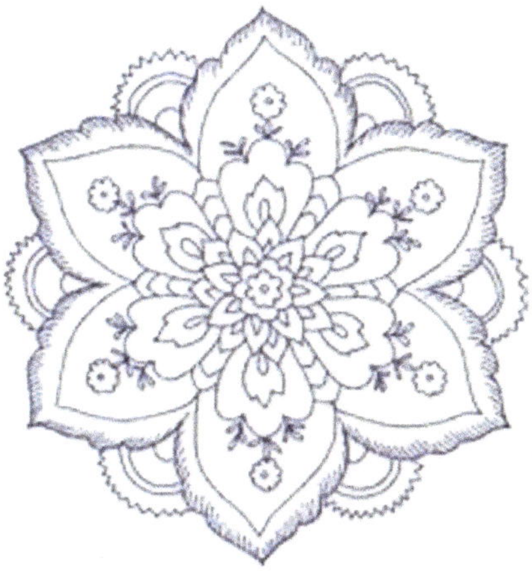

We all love Barbie..we do..
Yet this is what is really...true..
Would we love her the same..
If she looked like..the other..dame?
Beauty is in the eye of the beholder..

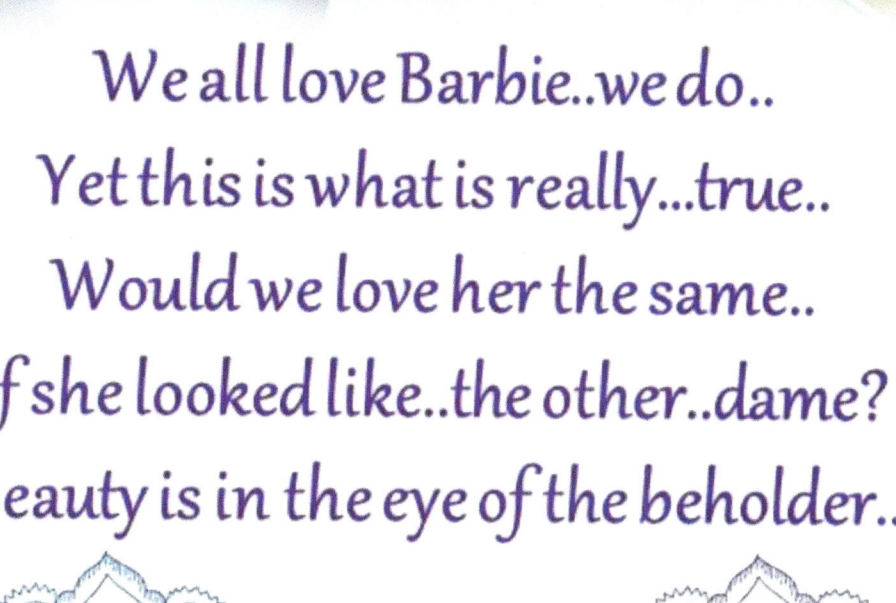

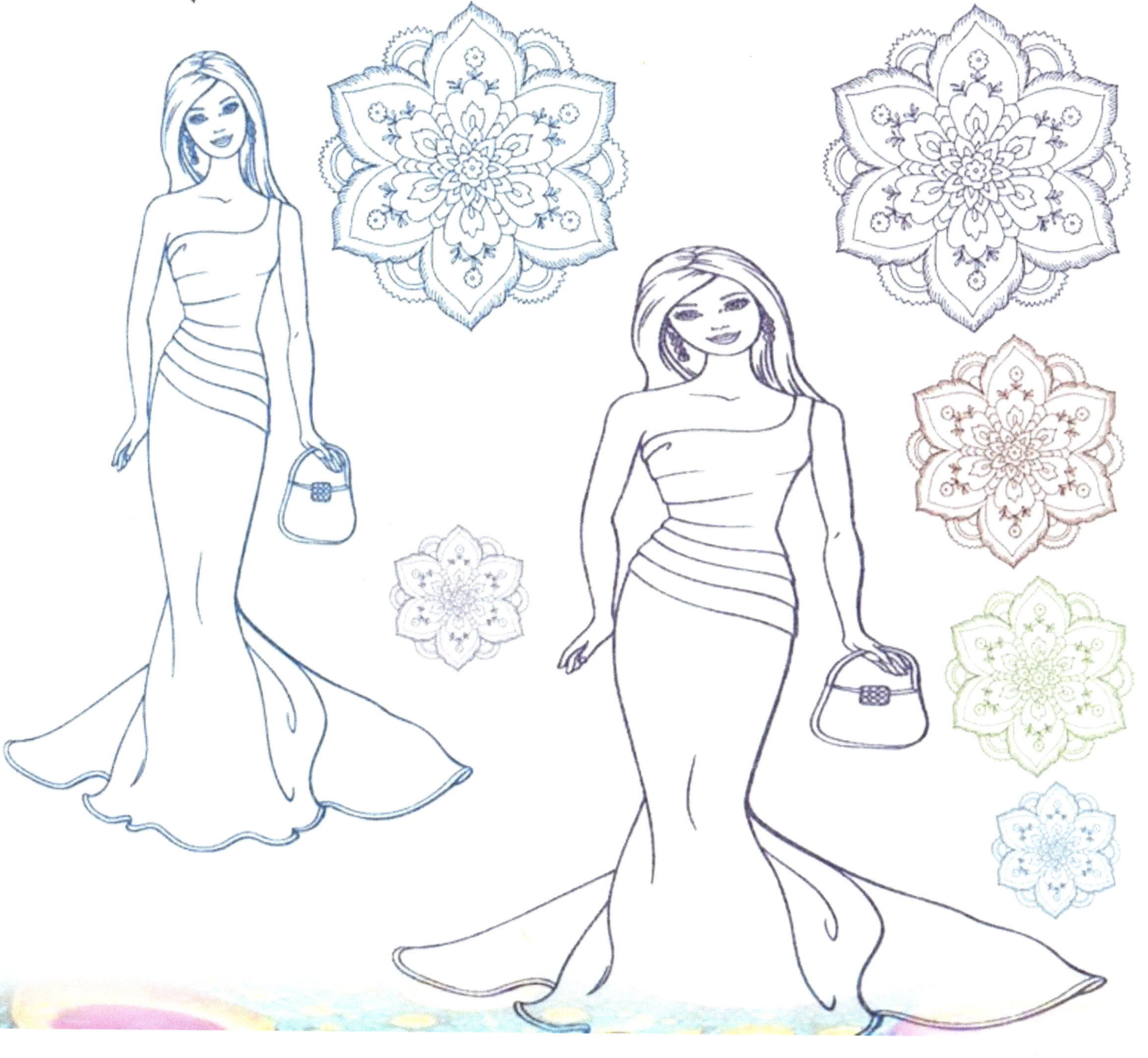

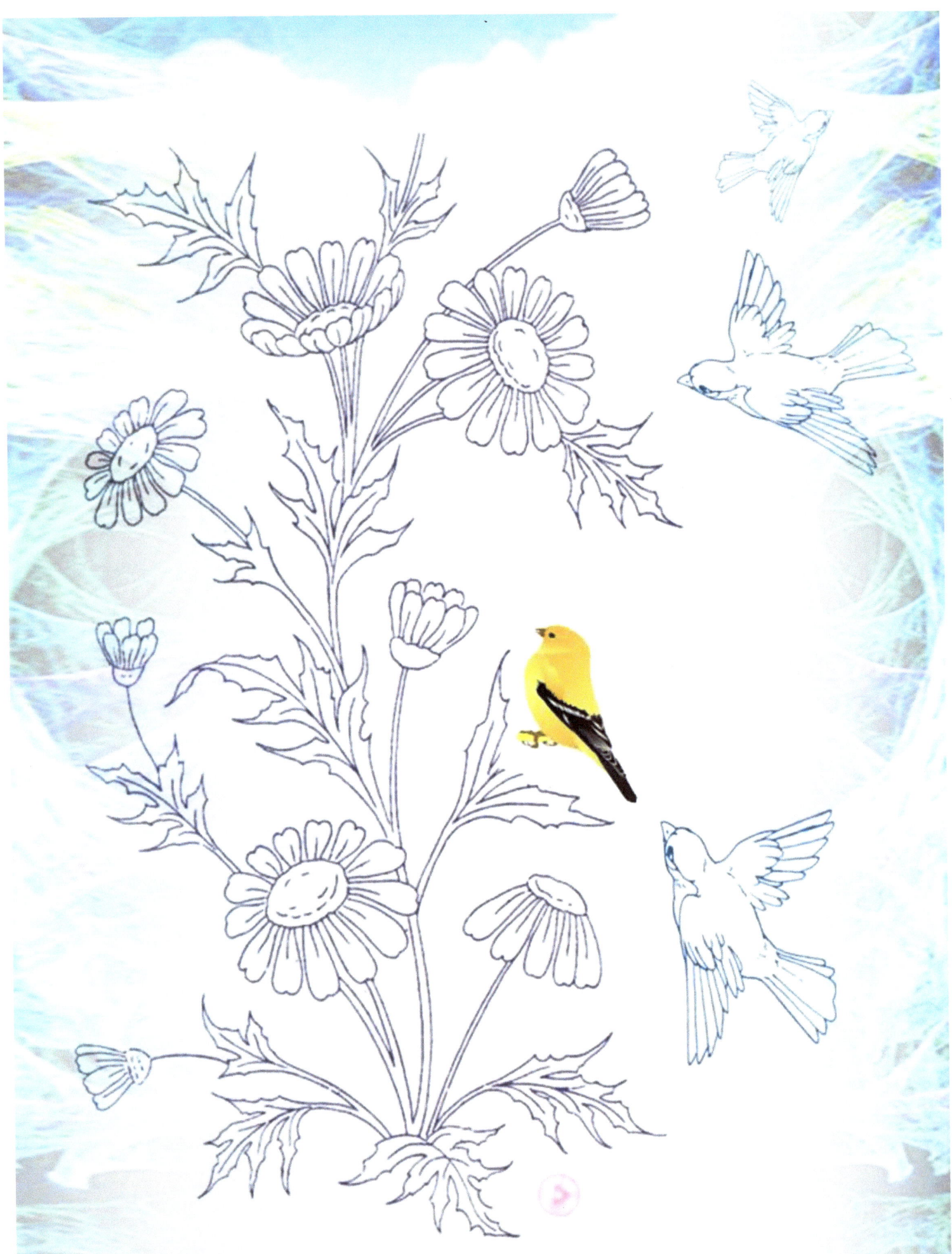

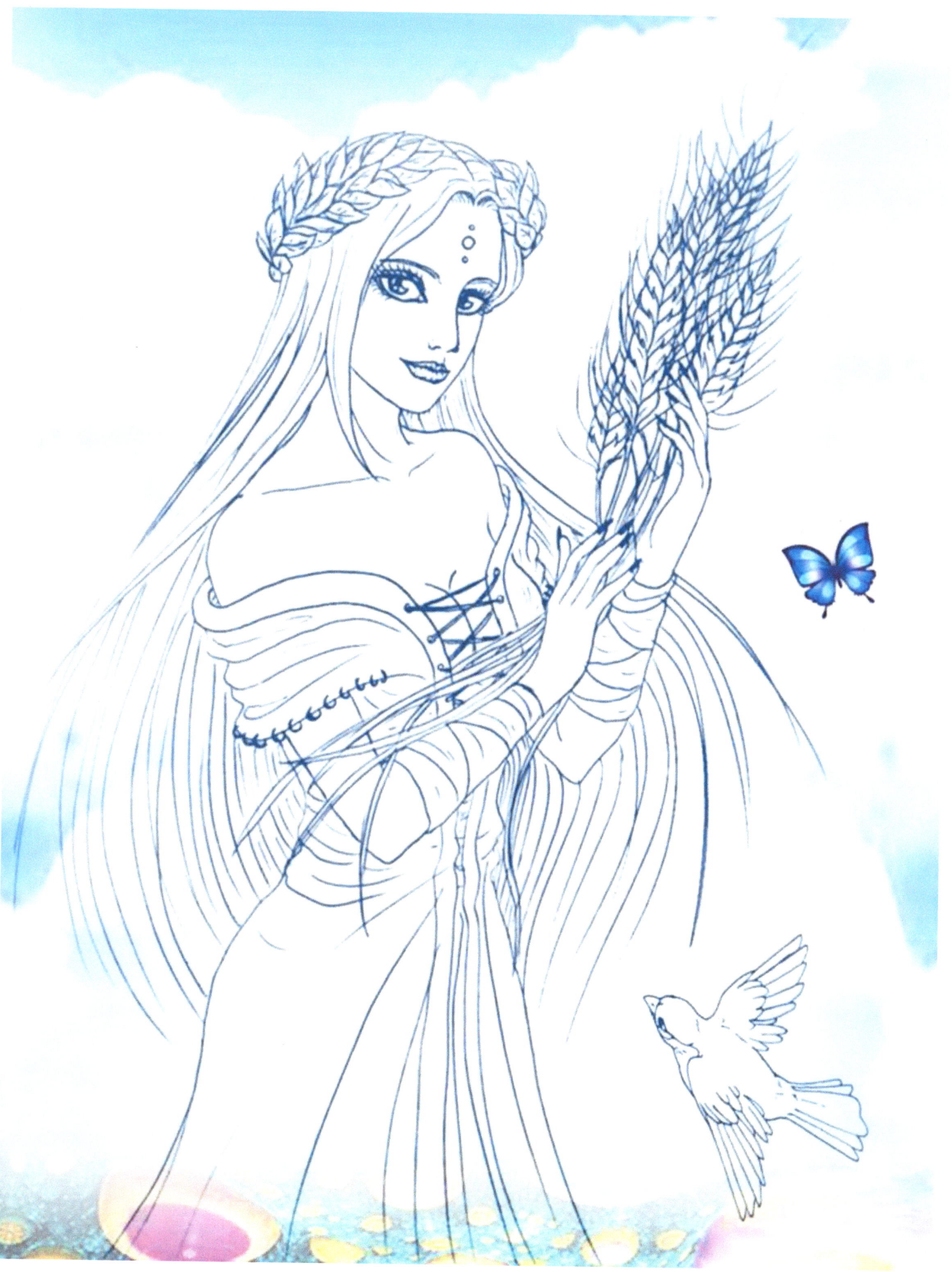

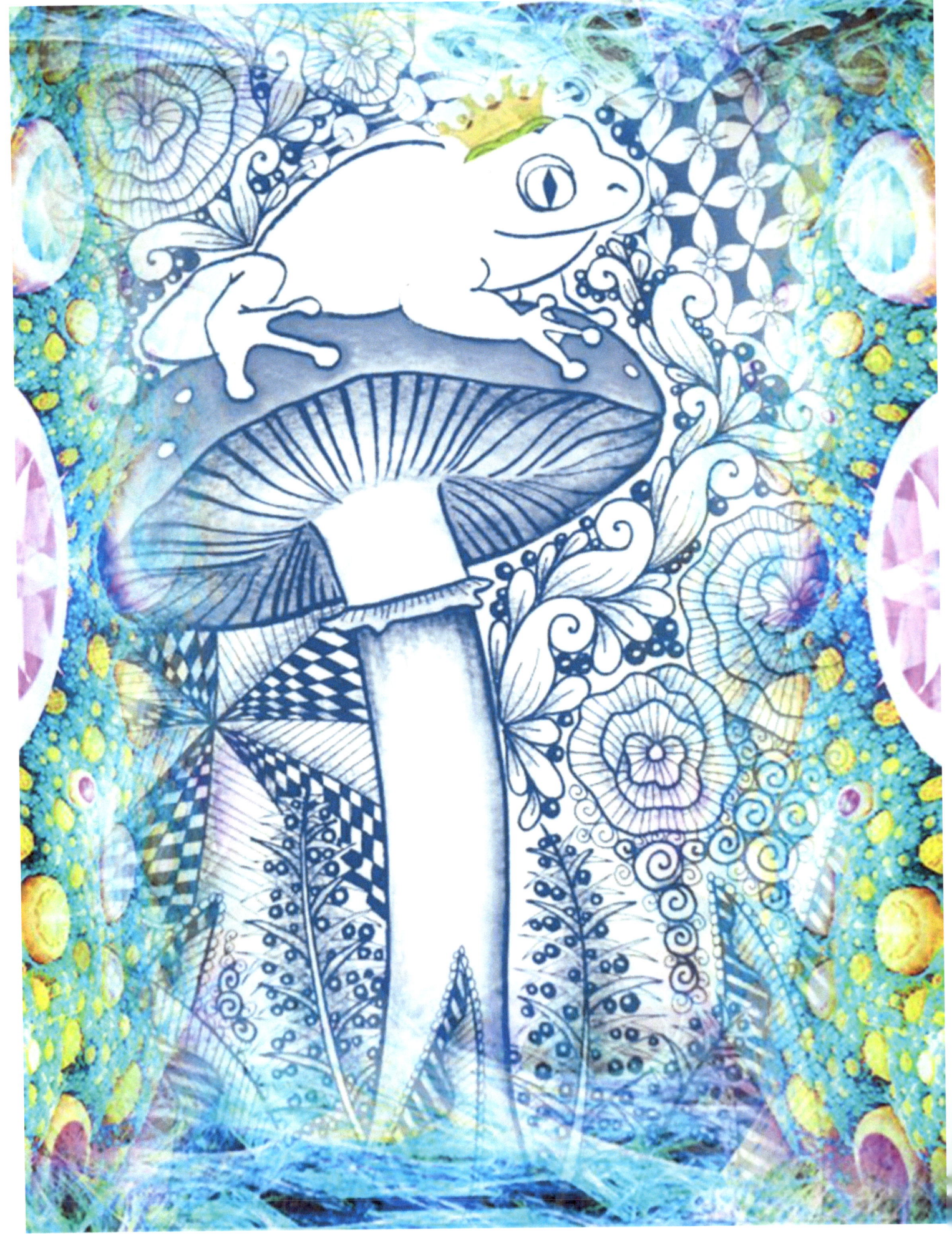

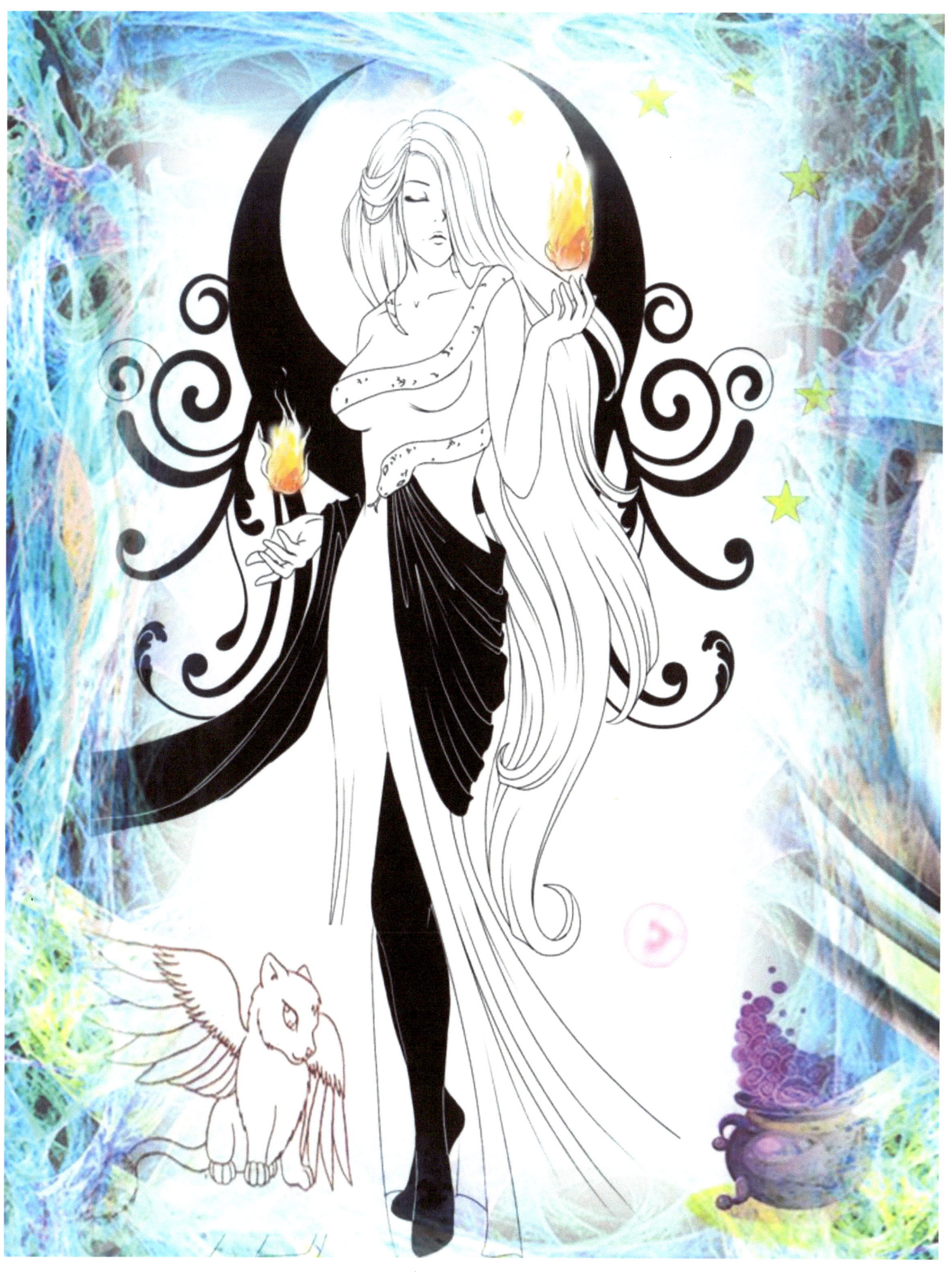

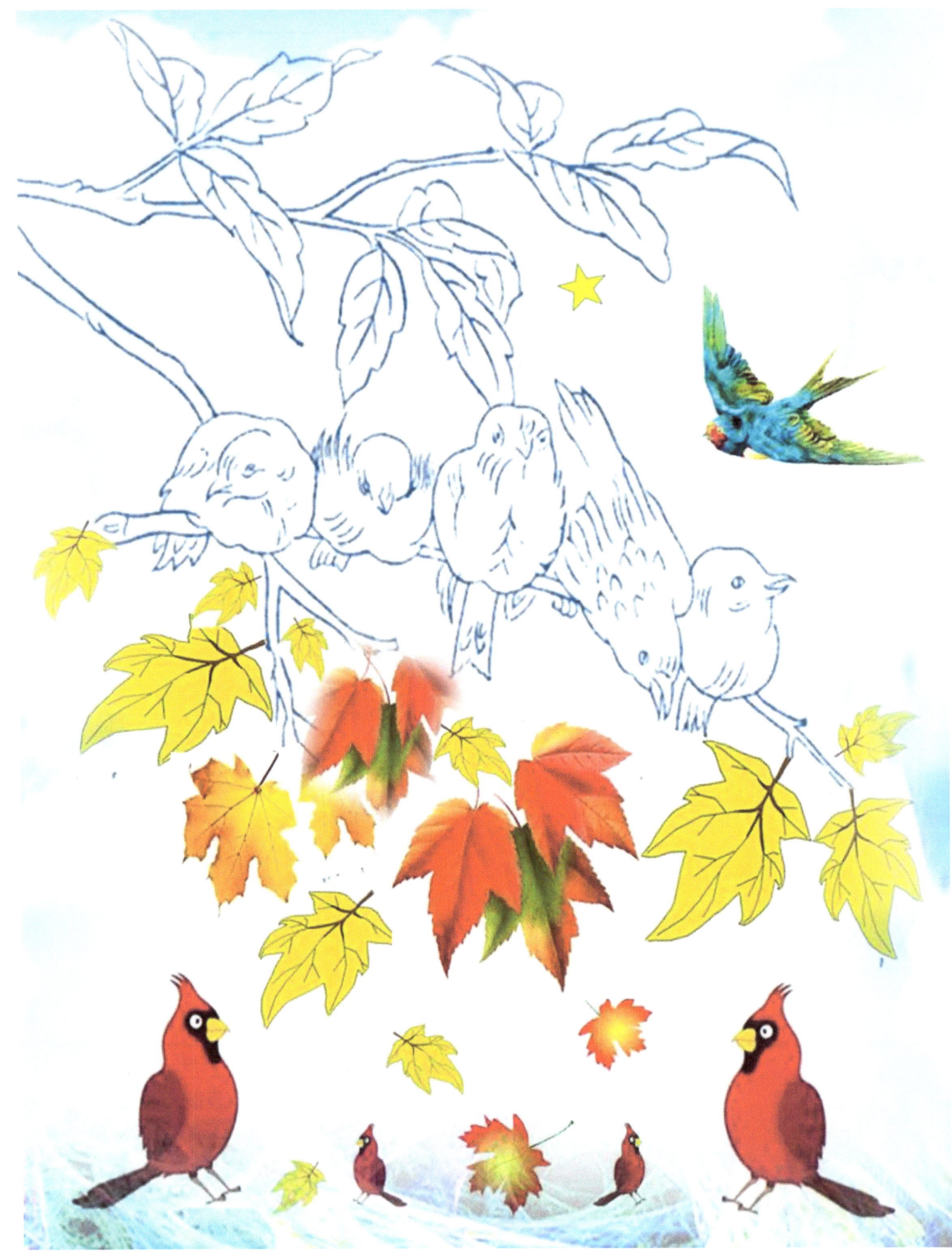

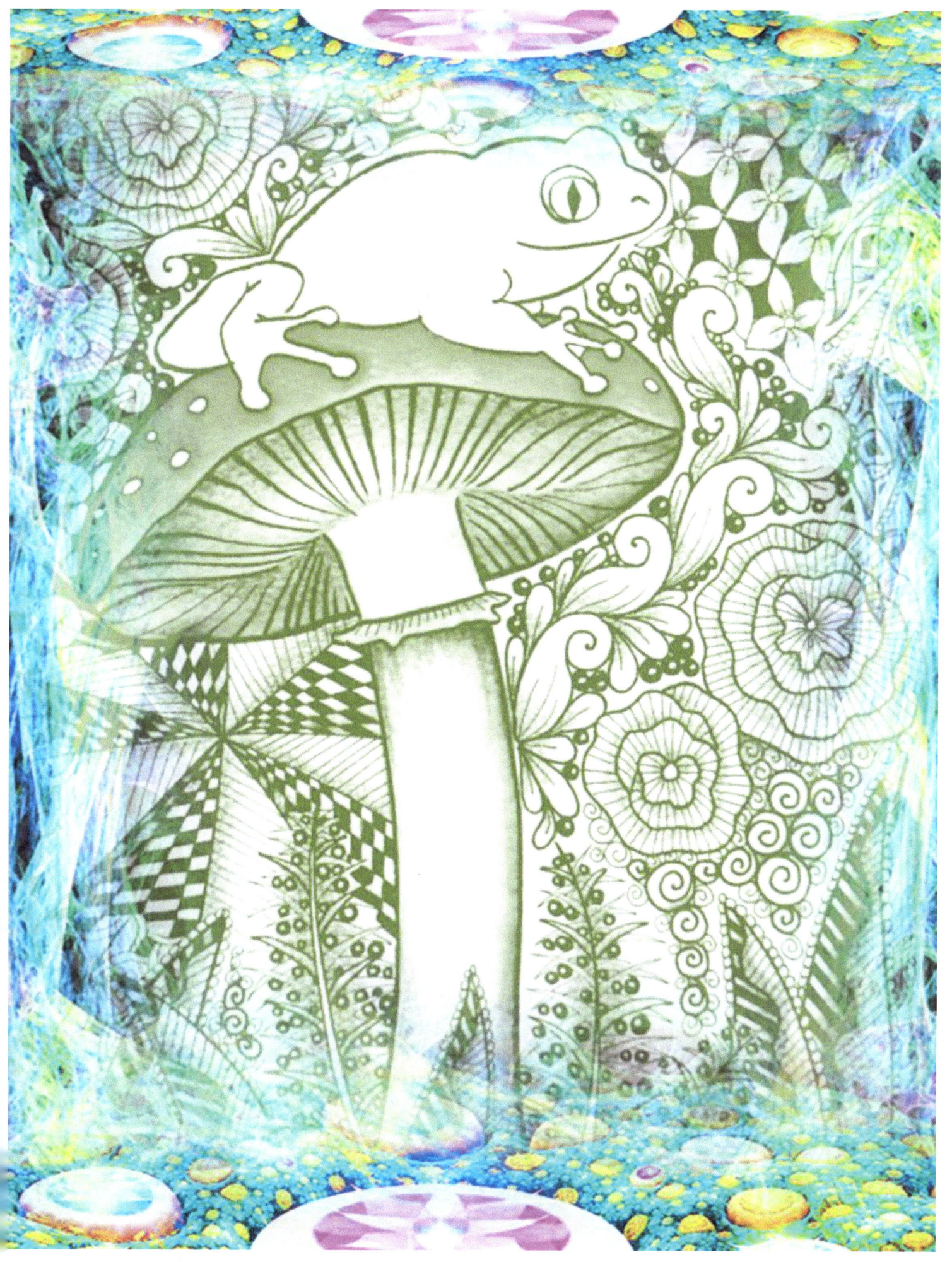

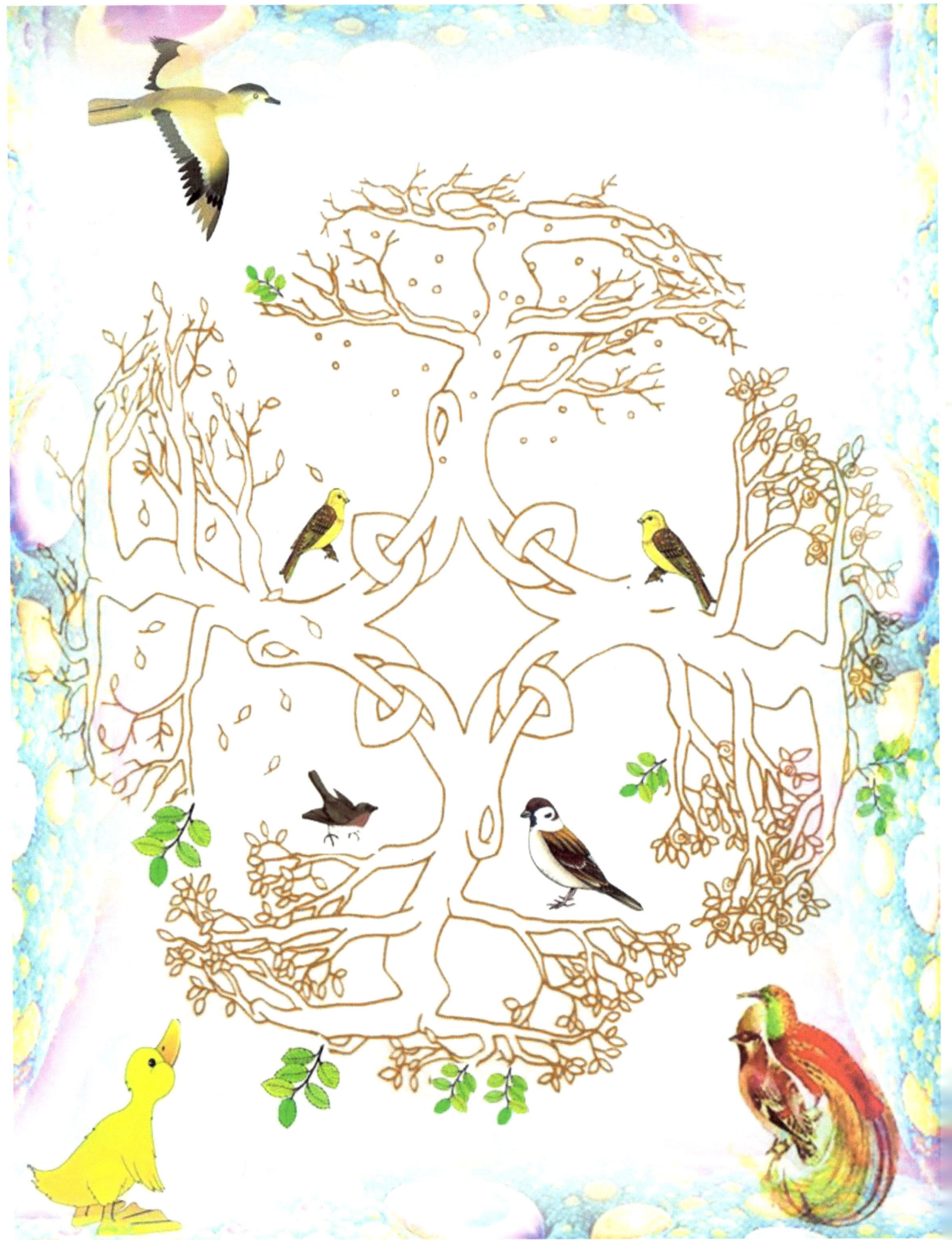

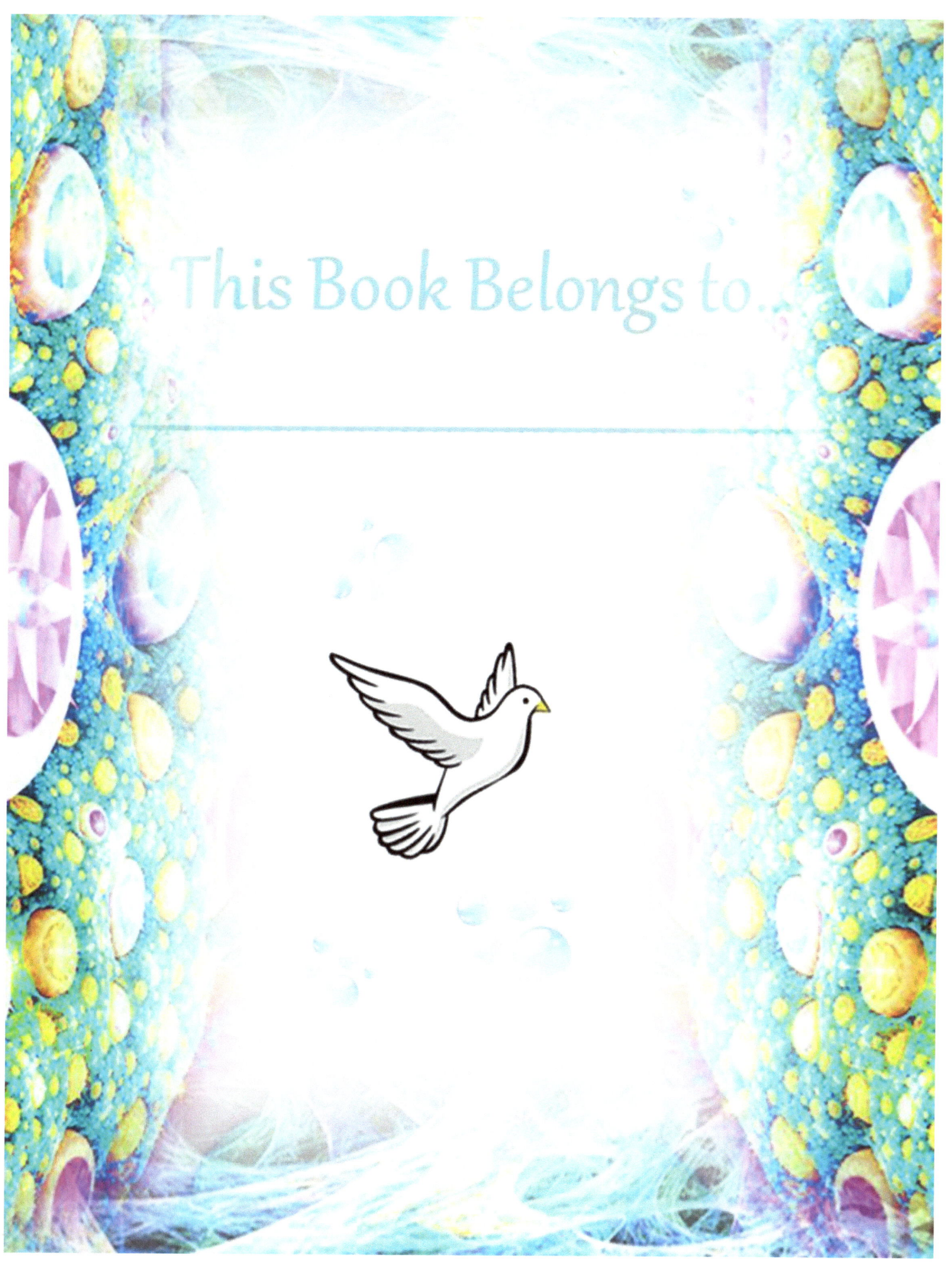

This Book Belongs to...

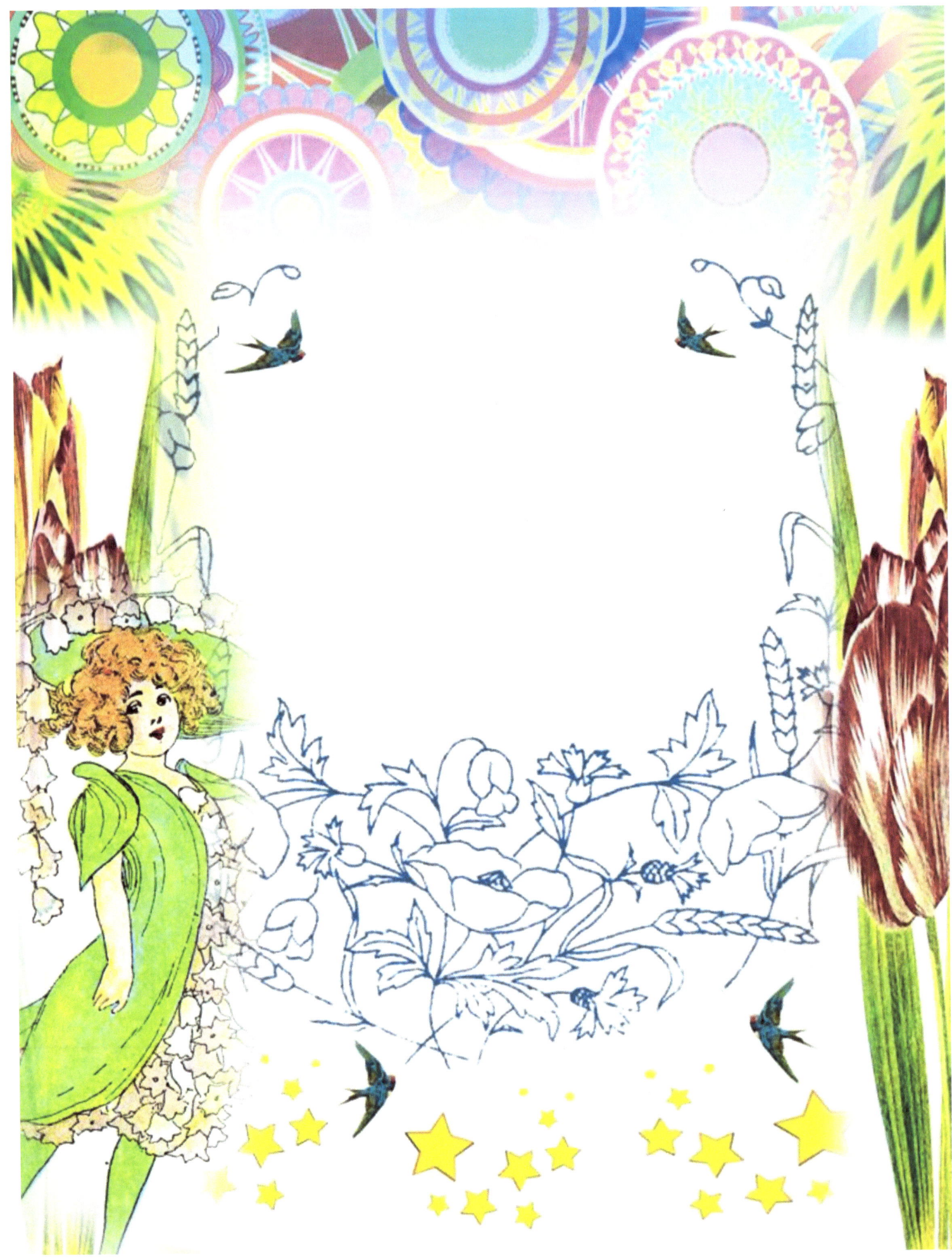

www.ingramcontent.com/pod-product-compliance
Lightning Source LLC
Chambersburg PA
CBHW050838180526

45159CB00004B/1943